I0098247

Jay's Administration Presents

Is My Fiancé Fucking Around?

A Novel by:

Jerome Staten

Is My Fiancé Fucking Around?

Published by Jay's Administration

Cover design by Jerome Staten

No part of this publication may be reproduced, stored in a retrieval system, or transmitted, in any form or by any means-electronic, mechanical, photocopying, recording, or otherwise- without prior written permission.

All Rights Reserved

Copyright 2011 by Jerome Staten

Printed In the United States of America

www.facebook.com/jeromestaten

Is My Fiancé Fucking Around?

Jerome Staten

Introduction

Decade after decade, while evolution precisely lives up to its assigned tasks of changing things completely from how we've grown accustomed to it being, one underlining factor remains the same, from coast-to-coast, someone's being cheated on.

For some, the signs of an unfaithful spouse, lingers right underneath their noses, giving off all types of warning/caution alerts to the party who's apparently left in the dark about their cheating partners.

Within this title, you'll have the opportunity to read up on what's taking place with four different couples, experiencing four different heart-wrenching scenarios, when they expose the dreadful conclusion that their loved ones, obviously has other objects of affection outside of the relationship/marriages.

The information provided within this book is not intended to offend anyone in any manner. All stories are based on real life actual events and it is being shared openly for informative educational purposes only.

Let's Begin . . .

Contents

The Concept of Cheating Shows No Remorse
~ Regardless of Your Gender ~

The concept of being unfaithful is a deceitful act that shows no prejudice intentions toward either gender, male or female; the heart-wrenching pain clenches tightly regardless of who you are, when the cheating party is exposed. From a man's perspective, his pride and dignity is immediately tarnished when he undoubtedly discovers that another man has violated his territory. The male's human mentality is that of a conqueror, a king of his domain, a dominant figure resembling a lion roaming the jungle or, a pedigree protecting the very yard that he frequents daily, the place he resides, his home.

For a female, she craves the manly affection, love and nurturing from her father as a kid growing up. When the dad is absent from her life, with no mutual bonding or connection at all, this leaves an enormous void in her life, leaving her vulnerable enough to seek this lack of attention from another man, as she grows and blossoms into a full-grown woman. As a result, she finds herself revisiting the same old dead-end routine with mostly every guy she allows into her life, because they're not completely fulfilling this unwanted void in her life either.

George & Miranda
~ *Life After Saying . . . I Do . . .* ~

Have you ever taken notice to how some relationships can last for over 10 years or longer but, as soon as the wedding vows are taken and the union is legally documented, the duration period of the marriage lasts way shorter than the long term relationship did? George and Miranda have been in love with one another ever since their college years back in the mid 90's, but, unfortunately for this couple, things seems to be taking a turn for the worse, not too long after their beautiful wedding reception.

"**B**abe, I have to admit," Miranda nervously explains, restlessly pacing back and forth across the living room's floor, glancing over at George to get her point across, "Although we've been in this relationship for over 12 years now, I'm nervous as shit about our wedding date tomorrow."

"What you're feeling is a natural reaction, hun," George responds, revealing the uneasiness he's harboring inside as well, "By the time our lips lock tomorrow afternoon, after we've exchanged rings and our wedding vows, the butterflies we're feeling in the pit of our stomachs right now, will vanish alongside the current title we have as just boyfriend and girlfriend."

"Honey, I know I've made you aware several times before how grateful I am to have you in my life and how genuinely appreciative I am of the way you've always accepted my sons, Kendal and Kevin, as if they're your own flesh and blood, George," Miranda weeps, hugging her tall, bulky fiancé tightly, as she leans her head against his chest. "I just love you way more than words can describe, sweetie."

"I take pleasure in loving and looking out for you and the boys, Miranda, you know this," George calmly exclaims, "If no one else realizes the pain you've endured from past relationships, I'm fully aware of the torture and turmoil your kids' father put you through before I stepped into your lives. That dude gave his all, not only to break your spirit with the physical abuse he constantly dished out, he also wanted to destroy your mental state-of-mind in the process; not to mention the drastic measures your sons had to endure witnessing those horrific encounters. When we first met, Miranda, you were no bigger than 105 pounds, soak and wet. You were extremely self conscious and very insecure about yourself. Now look at you, babe. You've put on weight in all the right places, you appear to be more confident in yourself and confident in what we have and, if I'm the cause of all of this, I'm honored more than you know."

"George, promise me that you'll always be this way toward me. Don't allow anyone or anything to ever cause you to have a change of heart. I've been through so much in my life already, my sons as well, and I honestly don't know what we'd do without you in our lives."

"Miranda, you have my word as your man that I'll never do anything, and I mean anything to hurt you or your sons, you see I haven't done so after all of these years. It would hurt me too much to see you guys in any more pain than you've already been through in life."

"Hey, Mr. George, do you feel like shooting some hoops today?" Kendal and Kevin asks, tossing their basketball back and forth to one another out on the patio area.

"I'll tell you guys what," George replies, kissing Miranda on the cheek, as he turns to give her sons his full attention, "How about we go around the corner to the park to shoot some hoops, instead of using this milk crate we have mounted on the garage's wall."

"Sounds good to me, Mr. George," Kendal replies, pulling his blue wrists band over his left arm, as if he's being called off the bench to play for a professional NBA team. "Wait until I show you the new trick shots I've learned, Kevin."

"First, I need you guys to straighten up that mess in your room before you go anywhere," Miranda laughs, lightly tapping her sons on their butts, as she's sending them off to their bedroom. "Make sure you're extra careful with them while you're at the park, George. You know how dangerous it is around there with all of that drug activity and all."

"Honey, they'll be just fine," George smiles, gently stroking Miranda's arm, "We'll be back before you know it."

After changing from his work attire into some around the house type of clothing, George and Miranda's sons are making their way to Central Park. The weather is fairly mild this evening, a slight break from the hounding humidity that has been pounding New York City this past week. Making sure he remains on the cool side, George is wearing his black and red colored thin material shorts, with a matching tank-top, revealing his defined muscular arms and chest.

"Say, Mr. George," Kevin curiously replies, "Why are we walking to the park instead of driving there in your Chevy Impala?"

"Ah, it's a long story, Kevin," says George, tilting his bottle of Gatorade back to quench his thirst, "I do miss driving my baby though. I remember when I first purchased her, as if it was yesterday. One day, both of you guys will be working on getting your licenses and, I'll be the first to tell you, it's no better feeling than having your license, guys. In my case, as a teenager, getting my license was the easy part. The part that I ran into trouble with was, getting a car."

"Cool, it looks like it's only a few people on the court today," Kendal replies, as his widening eyes are surveying the basketball court, the closer they're getting to Central Park.

Bypassing the hyper little kids that are running around freely on the grassy area of the park, George almost stumbles over a football that was mistakenly thrown toward his direction.

"Oops, I'm sorry, Sir," says one of the little boys, as he's approaching George to retrieve his football.

"Ah, don't worry about it, son," George smirks, tightly adjusting the football in the palm of his hand, as if he's about to launch it highly in the air for the kids to catch it, "Go deep toward that way."

Jogging back a few inches, adjusting his lengthy frame in a quarter-back stance, George notices a young lady near the swings, pushing a girl back and forth, which resembles his teenage daughter, Kayla.

"Are you coming, Mr. George?" Kendal and Kevin shouts from across the park, noticing that George has momentarily zoned-out in his own little world.

"Yeah, sorry guys," George replies, feet glued in place like a deer stuck in traffic, not knowing which way he should go, "Go ahead and get warmed up by taking a few practice shots. I'll be right over to join you in a sec."

Although things were extremely ugly in court earlier this year between George and his daughter's mother, Gina, over legal issues and a child support order pertaining to Kayla, George isn't allowing this to prevent him from going over to speak to his daughter. In court, George was initially there, seeking Joint Custody for Kayla, making his paternity rights just as equal as Gina's are. However, on that particular day, the only thing Judge Simmons appeared to be focused on was the large sum of back child support George apparently owed. It was perfectly clear that day that Judge Simmons had every intention of sending George to jail. Even though George was representing himself without any legal assistance like he was strongly advised to do, Judge Simmons still didn't really allow him get a word in edge wise when George attempted to get several lucrative points across. Like I said before, the only thing Judge Simmons saw that day was, George being in the arrears of owing over three thousand dollars in child support, when this large lump sum shouldn't have been accumulating to begin with.

However, by Gina receiving Social Services benefits and apparently doing all she can do to paint a perfect picture of George being the Non-Custodial Parent, when he's really not, has caused George to end up in this rocky boat for now.

"Hey, baby girl," George mutters, as he's walking closer to Kayla, while Gina's still gently pushing her on the swing, "How's daddy's baby girl doing today?"

Immediately beaming with excitement of seeing her dad, Kayla's smiling from ear to ear, as her hand progressively finds its way into the palm of George's hand.

"Well, hello to you too, George," Gina sarcastically rolls her eyes.

"Hey, Gina, how are you today?"

"I'm alive." Gina briefly responds with an attitude.

It's only been a minute and a half but, by the repeated smart slurs that are spewing from Gina's mouth, George is instantly reminded of one of his main reasons for leaving Gina in the first place.

"Why are you so grouchy all of the time, Gina?" George utters, glancing around at Miranda's sons on the basketball court, giving them a signal with his hand that he's on his way.

"Ah, I see you're having family day this evening, huh, George?" says Gina, looking over in the same direction as George, toward the basketball court. "Someone's missing from this picture though; I wonder where she could be."

"Miranda's home, Gina," George replies in a defensive tone, "But, I didn't come over here for that. I came to speak to my daughter and you as well, if your attitude wasn't so nasty."

"I don't have an attitude, sweetie, I just don't tolerate any bullshit."

"I'm not even going to argue with you, Gina," says George, kissing Kayla on the cheek before heading over to the basketball court with Kendal and Kevin, "I've been having a hard ass time lately, trying to find a job that has some stability though, because I'm so used to driving trucks for a living and I can't do so now for the simple fact that my license has been suspended due to that damn child support order you've caused.

"The child support order that I've caused," Gina loudly responds, "Did you think you were going to just get by without paying any child support, George? You and I might not be in a relationship anymore, but, that doesn't mean Kayla doesn't need some financial assistance on your behalf."

"Are you fucking kidding me, Gina," George replies in a shocked tone, "I take damn good care of Kayla financially and you know it. You're just doing this shit to try to make my life as miserable as yours is, that's all this is about."

"You know what," Gina frustratingly mumbles, urgently gathering Kayla's belongings, as she assisting Kayla off of the swing, "I'm not going to stand here and listen to you talk shit, George. Always remember though, all because you're fucking another woman, doesn't mean I don't have control over your ass. Trust me when I tell you this."

Irate at the fact that he even parted his lips to participate in Gina's systematic trap of an on-going argument, George is rushing back over to the basketball court to let off some steam.

"Is everything all right?" Kendal replies, noticing that George seems to be a little bit more somber than he was earlier.

"Oh, definitely guys," says George, knowing deep down inside he's as pissed as any human being can be, "Everything is just fine."

George, Kendal and Kevin played multiple rounds of the basketball game known as, H-O-R-S-E, up until the street lights were moments away from flashing on, symbolizing the arrival of the night time. Arriving back home, after stopping at the gas station and the local 7-Eleven to pick up a couple of slurpees, nothing's being said by Kendal and Kevin about George spending a few minutes conversing with Kayla's mom at the park.

"All right, guys, I'll see you in the morning," says George, heading in the opposite direction of Kendal and Kevin, proceeding toward the bathroom.

"Did you two enjoy yourselves out on the basketball court this evening?" Miranda replies, glancing around at her sweaty sons, as she's patiently anticipating an answer.

Tempted to make Miranda aware right now that they weren't the only ones that George spent some time with this evening, Kevin and Kendal are doing the complete opposite instead.

"Yep, we had a ball, mom," Kevin responds, eventually followed up by Kendal delivering the same identical confirmation.

"Well, I'm glad to hear that," says Miranda, neatly folding her flower-printed apron, as she's placing it on top of the washing machine, "Go ahead and get washed up for dinner so you guys can eat and then head to bed."

From the distant, far-out look that Miranda's eyes possess right now, it's perfectly obvious that she's feeling as though something isn't right. Any other time, Kendal and Kevin would come home ramping and raving about the tons of fun they had while being out somewhere with George. Tonight, they've been brief and very limited when it comes to describing the events that occurred while they were out. This weird feeling that Miranda's experiencing in the pit of her stomach right now, has surpassed the nervous feeling she had earlier about her wedding tomorrow. It's almost as if she's been here before; never with George but, in a past relationship when she was being cheated on.

However, Miranda's blocking these unwanted feelings out momentarily, as she's heading toward the bedroom to go to sleep.

"I love you baby," George replies, giving Miranda a goodnight kiss on the cheek, the moment he climbs into bed with her.

Cradling himself closely behind Miranda in bed, wrapping his strong arms around her, pulling her closer to him, George quietly whispers in Miranda's ear,

"This time tomorrow night, we'll be husband and wife, babe."

Within those few little words alone, Miranda has found the significance in them enough to enable it to block out any odd feelings she's been experiencing within lately. Tomorrow is her wedding day and nothing or no one is going to ruin it for her.

The following afternoon, at Mount Calvert's Church, family members and friends have gathered together to celebrate the union between George and Miranda, as a newly wedded couple. As promised by George, the nervous energy that he and Miranda felt just yesterday, prior to getting married, has vanished like a dark green colored leaf in autumn.

"Do you, George Milton Stevenson, take Miranda as your lawfully wedded wife, to love and to cherish, through sickness and in health, 'til death do you part?" says Pastor Miller, as he stands before the crowded church.

"I do," George proudly responds, holding Miranda's hand firmly in his, sliding the beautiful ring on her finger, as he's staring directly into her welling eyes.

"Miranda Mitchell, do you take George as your lawfully wedded husband, to love and to cherish, through sickness and in health, 'til death do you part?"

"I most certainly do!" Miranda grins, reaching down to slide George's ring on his finger.

"With the power vested in me," Pastor Miller continues, "I now pronounce you man and wife; you may now kiss your bride."

"We did it babe," Miranda gleefully smiles at George, hugging him tightly, as they're entwining in a long passionate kiss. "We're actually husband and wife now!"

"Indeed we are," George loudly laughs, as he's guiding Miranda, Kendal and Kevin out of the congested church.

By this being their honeymoon night, a night that's full of promised possibilities and countless unforgettable moments, Miranda asked her mom, Cathy, sometime last week, if it was ok if Kendal and Kevin spent the weekend with her. This alone time with her new husband, George, is long over-due and, Miranda is hell bent on enjoying every lasting second of it.

 The first two years of George and Miranda's marriage couldn't be better. George maintained the same respect level and loving ways that he's always had toward Miranda and her sons. However, nothing in life is perfect and this very statement doesn't exclude George and Miranda either.

Late one night, while waiting on the bus stop for a bus that doesn't appear to be showing up anytime soon, George is deciding to use the last few dollars he has in his pocket, to pay for a cab.

"This shit here is fucking ridiculous," George mutters within, "I have to get my license back as soon as possible because, this nickel and diming it, catching buses and cabs every day, is literally taking its toll on my pockets. I'd still be making a whole lot of cash if I was driving trucks like I used to do."

On his way home in the coziness of the Diamond Cab he's flagged down, George's mind has drifted off, picturing the provoking appearance he remembers from the look on Gina's face whenever he saw her. As much as he hates to admit it, one statement that Gina constantly made over and over again, appears to be true; she does have a huge amount of power over him with that child support order.

There has to be a way to get things back on a leveled playing field again, when it comes to Gina's greedy, spiteful ass, sponging up all of the money from child support, whenever it's being paid by George; George just hasn't figured out the key strategy yet. In the back of his wandering mind, George realizes that, it'll always be one way that he could stop the child support order. He's just fully aware that it'll be a heftier price tag to pay with Miranda, if he did follow up on these random thoughts he's having of breaking a sacred promise he's made, as well as damaging the wedding vows he took two years ago. George is basically stuck between a rock and a hard place and it's been this way for years now.

Finally arriving home for the evening, George is tiresomely walking over to greet his wife, who appears to have just hung up the phone.

"Hey, honey, I didn't hear you come in," says Miranda, extending her loving arms out to receive her bulky husband, "My sister, Karen, just asked about you."

"Oh yeah," George replies, pulling back the aluminum foil that's covering his plate of food, so he can see what Miranda prepared for dinner tonight, "How have things been with Karen lately, is she still involved with the guy that she was seeing; I believe his name is, Larry, or something like that?"

"It's, Leonard, but, yes, they're still involved, babe."

"Ah, that's great honey; Karen needs a good man in her life because of how good she is to other people."

"She sure does, babe," Miranda replies, "Are you all right though, you seem to be down this evening, George?"

"Oh, yeah, I'm good, babe," George slightly grins, "Just had another long ass day working for this temp agency that I'm working for, that's all. By the way, where's Kevin and Kendal, I didn't see them when I came in?"

"They should be home in any minute now," says Miranda, "Their uncle, Tommy, took them to the mall today to buy them a few things since he haven't seen them in so long."

"Tommy," George confusingly frowns, taking another bite of his mouth-watering chicken breast, as he's glancing around at Miranda, "Where do I know him from?"

"You're so silly, babe," Miranda playfully taps George on the arm, "Tommy is my cousin on my father's side, the one I told you about that lives in North Carolina."

Not being able to recall right away of Miranda mentioning Tommy before, George is shrugging his shoulders, sampling a fork of Miranda's macaroni and cheese, as he questions,

"Did I receive any mail today, babe?"

"Just the normal stuff," Miranda explains, "Our monthly cable bill, a letter sent to the wrong address and, some junk mail."

"All right babe," George replies, placing the remainder of his food in the refrigerator, as he's turning to proceed down the darkened hallway, "Tell the boys I said, hey, whenever they come in. I'm beat tonight so, I'm heading to bed now."

"Ok, baby, I sure will," says Miranda, peeping through the curtains to see if her sons are outside yet, "I'll be in there shortly to join you."

A half hour later, after George has fallen fast asleep and Miranda damn near drifted off herself while she's curled up on the loveseat in the living room, Kevin and Kendal arrives at the front door, turning to wave at Tommy, who chose to remain in his car this time.

"All right, boys, I'll see you the next time!" Tommy yells out from his car.

"It's about time you guys got here," Miranda yawns, standing back against the wall, holding the front door opened wide enough for Kevin and Kendal to get in, "I thought I was going to have to come out to look for you two!"

"Look at the new video game we got, mom," Kevin excitedly replies, holding the PlayStation 3 game up in the air for Miranda to see it, "Is Mr. George still awake, I want to show him this new basketball game we got?"

"No, George is fast asleep, Kevin," says Miranda, clenching her silk night gown together with her left hand, "You can show it to him tomorrow though when he wakes up."

"Ok, cool," says Kevin.

"Did you guys eat while you were at the mall, Kendal?"

"Yes, we had a couple slices of pizza and some fries."

"Mmmm, sounds good," Miranda grins, "It's late now boys so, go ahead and wash up for bed."

"All right, mom," Kevin replies, showing Kendal the features on the back cover of the game, as they're heading toward their bedroom.

Bright and early the next day, Kevin and Kendal are eagerly anticipating the appearance of George, so they can show him this video game that they've been dying to get.

"Hey, guys," says George, as he's walking into the spacious kitchen to pour a tall glass of Tropicana orange juice, "How are you feeling this morning?"

"We're great, Mr. George," Kevin and Kendal simultaneously responds, "Do you want to play us in this basketball game we got last night when you come home from work today?"

"Sure, guys, let me see what you've got there," says George, reaching out to receive the video game from Kendal, "Ahh, NBA 2012, I definitely want to play you in this game later on, after I stop at the Barbershop to get my hair cut."

"Yes!" Kendal and Kevin clinches their fists in the air, highly ecstatic about George accepting their invitation to join them later in some grueling PlayStation 3 basketball action.

"You guys be good, kiss your mom for me when she wakes up and, I'll see you later on," George utters, adjusting his pin-striped neck tie around his neck, as he's reaching down to pick his sunglasses up off the counter before heading out into the world.

Making it a few blocks away from his house, about another block or so away from the bus stop, George notices that his Singular One, prepaid cell phone is vibrating.

"What the hell," George surprisingly replies, with a perplexed look upon his face, as he's removing his headphones to receive Gina's call, "Gina's actually calling me; I wonder what this is all about."

In the past, Gina's random phone calls always meant that another argument wasn't too far behind. Things had gotten so bad between these two that, George was left with no other alternative other than to ignore Gina's calls, especially since they weren't pertaining to Kayla.

"Hello," George replies, listening closely to what Gina is about to say.

"Hey, daddy, this is Kayla, hold on for a second, my mommy wants to speak to you."

"George, listen," Gina begins, "I'm not calling to argue with you or anything, I just wanted to know if you could stop by my place whenever you get a chance, to fix the broken thermostat. I don't know anyone else that knows how to fix it but, it's hot as hell in here and your daughter needs to be in a cool environment because of the asthma she has. If you can't do it, that's fine, just let me know."

At this point, George has every intention of telling Gina that it serves her right that she's burning up in her apartment. This woman is seriously demon possessed and if she continues on being the way that she is now, her ass will be residing in the type of heat for eternity that'll have no options of having a thermostat fixed to cool her off. Kayla's the only reason why George didn't follow up on his initial thoughts of telling Gina where she can go. Kayla's living in that same apartment as well and needs the air, even more so than Gina does. Plus, maybe this favor for Gina will be a golden opportunity to switch gears, eliminating the child support order so he can finally get his license back.

"Well, you know, Gina," George begins to negotiate, "I'm unable to drive now so, it'll be extremely difficult for me to get over there after work today.

"George, I'll pay your cab fare," Gina replies, shaking her head even though George is unaware of it, "I'd offer you a ride myself but, I wouldn't want your precious little wife to somehow find out about you being in my car, "Trust me when I tell you, as much trust as you think that Miranda has in you, that shit would be tested to the fullest if she knew we were riding around town together. All I need is my air fixed though, nothing more nothing less."

"All right, Gina," George reluctantly replies, "I'll try to stop by after work today, just to fix your air, but, nothing else."

"Child, please," says Gina, "That's all I want from you anyway is for you to fix my air."

Meanwhile, back at the house, Miranda has awakened now and she's in progress of following up on her same ole daily routine of being a stay-at-home wife and mom. Miranda has been disabled some time now, preventing her from going out into the work force like George does, every since the car accident occurred 3 years ago, permanently damaging her left leg, causing her to limp when she walks. By Miranda not being able to work, only receiving a disability check once a month, puts a strenuous amount of financial pressure on George to be the sole provider. Bills are barely being paid now because of this one-sided ordeal. However, George wakes up every morning, sick or not and heads out into the world to provide for his family, with his head held high, regardless of how stressed out he may be.

"Hey, little kitty-cat," Miranda softly whispers, bending over to pour some cat food into Buttons' cat bowl, "Mommy has to get her baby some more food later on because you're running out."

Gently brushing up against Miranda's leg, closing her eyes as she's sticking her head up for Miranda to rub it, Buttons eventually walks over toward the area where her food and milk is, and begins eating and drinking.

"Geez, I need to do something with this head of mines," says Miranda, looking at herself in the mirror, as she's removing the pink-colored hair rollers.

Miranda has the prettiest, milk chocolate type of skin that anyone has ever seen. Whenever she wears make-up, which she only does on special occasions, all it does is heighten her immaculate beauty even more. Even though Miranda's complaining about her hair right now while she's looking in the mirror, in all actuality, it's really nothing wrong with it. True, Miranda doesn't have a professional hair salon type of style right now but, her lengthy hair is naturally beautiful without one.

Reaching down to place the last roller inside the plastic bag, Miranda is startled by a sudden knock on her front door.

"Hmmm, I wonder who this can be this time of the day," says Miranda, attentively looking over at the clock that's mounted on the kitchen's wall to see what time it is.

Nervously extending her shivering hand out to turn the knob of the front door, Miranda quietly utters,

"Who is it?"

Not receiving a response after the 1st three tries, Miranda's slowly screeching the door opened, peeping out to see if anyone is on her steps. In this case, this is one of the times that Miranda wishes she would've just ignored the knocking on the door sound, at least until George was home with her.

"Hey, honey, I'm home," Kendal and Kevin's biological father, Mitch replies, as he's greeting a completely stunned Miranda. "You look surprised to see me, sweetness."

For Miranda, surprised is an understatement to the 3rd degree. The last time Miranda actually saw Mitch, face to face, was when Mitch was going upside her head a long time ago, and the police came out to escort this abusive beast away. Time obviously flew by since that dreadful night for Miranda, because she honestly had no clue that Mitch would be released from prison anytime soon.

"Say, love, where are our boys," Mitch arrogantly replies, noticing that same fearful look in Miranda's eyes that he used to capitalize on in the past, "I know they're all big and grown up now, aren't they?"

"Kendal and Kevin are in school right now, Mitch," Miranda jittery mutters, "Say, I don't think it's a good idea for you to be here right now though, so, please leave."

"It's not a good time?" Mitch replies in a deep toned voice. "Leave it up to you, Miranda; it'll never be a good time."

"Just leave, Mitch, I don't want any trouble."

"I'll leave for now, honey," Mitch wickedly laughs, holding his foot in the door to prevent Miranda from closing it, "Trust and believe though; I will be back for you and our boys."

Completely relieved that Mitch left this time without putting up a fight, but simultaneously disheartened to the fact that he's actually back on the streets again as a free man, Miranda just slithered down onto the floor near the front door, clenching her chest tightly, as tears of fear streams down her face. Seeing Mitch's stern looking face again, up close and personal, immediately informs Miranda that, without a shadow of a doubt, her life as she knows it to be right now, is about to experience hell right here on earth. Mitch isn't going to go away without putting up a fight, even though he just left with no problems a minute ago. To make matters worse, Miranda shares kids with this man and who's to say that Kendal and Kevin wouldn't want to forgive their father, ultimately giving him a 2nd chance at being a part of their lives. If this is the case, we'll have to sit back and observe how George responds to it. For over a decade now, George has been the only dad that Kendal and Kevin have ever known.

However, George has a kid outside of this marriage with Miranda as well, and as we speak, George is only a few blocks away from Gina's house now to fix her thermostat unit as promised.

"The unit is right over there, George," Gina points toward the corner of the apartment, showing George where the thermostat unit is located, "As you can see, all its doing is blowing out hot air."

"Hey, Kayla," George smiles, reaching down to hug his daughter, who've just wrapped her loving arms around him, "How are you doing today, sweetheart?"

"I'm ok, daddy, just hot," Kayla softly replies.

"Well, your dad is going to have you cooled off in one sec," says George, reaching down inside the leather tool belt that's wrapped around his waist, searching for the proper tools needed for this task.

"So, George, how is the married life treating you," says Gina, comfortably positioning her smooth, oiled-up glistening legs on the sofa, as she's lying back watching television, "Is she everything you dreamed she would be?"

"Here you go again," George replies, forcefully twisting a screw with his screw driver, seemingly almost done fixing the thermostat unit, "You're all up in my marriage when you should be focused on you and your relationship."

"Ha, you're funny," Gina sarcastically blurts out, "Besides, if I was in a relationship and wanted to be bothered with a man, do you think I'd have you over here fixing the air for me?"

"Yes, I sure do," George boastfully sticks his chest out, extremely proud of the fact that he's one of the only men in this neighborhood that's very handy and skillful with fixing things, "You would have to hire a contractor to fix something like this and, I know you wouldn't."

"Yeah, ok," Gina utters, reaching down to shrug Kayla's shoulder, waking her up so she can go in her bedroom to lay down, "Kayla, come on baby, it's time to go in your room so you can go to sleep."

"My baby girl is tired I see," George turns around to reply, "She fell asleep on the floor while watching Tyler Perry's movie."

"I finally feel a little bit of air blowing out now," Gina yells out from Kayla's bedroom, "I see you do know what you're doing, huh?"

"Of course I do," George loudly responds, lowering the thermostat at a cooler temperature to see if his job is successfully complete.

"Well, I surely do appreciate it," says Gina, as she's returning to the living room area, "It was miserable as hell in here without my air."

"Say, come to think of it," George utters, confidence level of being one of the only men in the neighborhood that's good with his hands, diminishing as he speaks, "This is your landlord's responsibility, Gina, to fix things in your apartment that's not working properly. Why didn't you report it to him so he could send a maintenance man out instead of you having to call me; you still wouldn't be paying anything either way?"

Seductively walking over toward George, hand lowered as if she's about to palm George's penis through his pants, Gina softly whispers,

"I thought I'd give you a fair chance at giving me what I need and in exchange, we'd work something out pertaining to the child support order that has you in debt."

Totally stunned at this point, not knowing what he should say or, what rash decision he should make right here on the spot, George's back is firmly against the living room's wall, mouth widened really wide, but nothing is coming out of it.

"You said you need your license back in order to make a decent living driving trucks, right," Gina continues, passionately nibbling on George's right earlobe, as her sinful hand slides underneath George's shirt, "Why not give me what I need whenever I request it and, we can work on making sure your license is back in your possession again?"

George is undeniably on the verge right now of violating every single word and promise he made to Miranda in the past. The stakes are extremely heavy right now because, he needs his license back more than anything. He's nowhere close to having the amount of money needed to pay his back child support, getting the suspension lifted from his driver's license, enabling him to quit working for the dead-end temp agency he's with now. Not only is Gina the key method he thought of before, that plays a huge part in this child support dilemma, she's also one of the only women who can make George weak in the knees with the slightest touch, regardless of how much of a headache she is at times.

The flesh is weak, George's mind is racing a mile a minute, but, through all of this, even while pinned firmly in the corner of the impactful amount of pressure that this type of temptation has over a human being, George has somehow mustered up enough dignity to push Gina's hand aside, as he utters,

"I can't do this, Gina, I can't cheat on my wife; I love her too much."

"You're a fucking fool, George," Gina embarrassingly jerks away, "Here I am, offering you access to the pussy whenever you want some, regardless of your marital status and you're rejecting it! I guess you don't want your damn license back too badly after all. We can let shit between us remain exactly how it is now, since it's like that. I don't know any fucking man that would turn down the offer of being able to fuck another woman, even while he's married."

"You're looking at one now, Gina," George boldly replies, picking his tool belt up off the floor, as he's proceeding toward the front door, "I know it'll take me a long ass time to come up with the money I need to pay off the child support I owe, leading me to getting my license back. Hell, they're already garnishing any amount of money I'm getting as a refund during income tax season and the little bit of money I'm making at my job. I'm damn near on the verge of going to jail because of this shit, but, I'll find a way to get back on track. Cheating on my wife in order to get these things done just isn't an option for me. I'm not the man I used to be, Gina."

"Fuck it then," Gina irately replies, slamming the door behind George, "I don't need to fuck your trifling ass. I can get some dick anytime I want it!"

Using the few dollars he got from Gina for cab fare before she became so annoyed with him, George is heading home now, with no intentions of making Miranda aware of where he's been.

"Mom, Mr. George promised he'd play the game with us when he got home tonight," Kevin replies, realizing that Miranda is about to make him and Kendal go to bed, "Can we stay up a little while longer to see him when he comes in?"

"Kevin, I said it's time for bed now," Miranda sternly replies, storing the last few dishes away that she just finished drying off, "Now go on, you two have school tomorrow and it's getting late."

Reluctantly turning the video game off, Kendal and Kevin are disappointingly heading toward their bedroom, both boys appearing to have a frown on their faces.

By the time George arrived home tonight, Miranda has already made her way to bed. On her side of the bed, Miranda's dealing with the depressing, horrific feeling inside, of trying to find ways to explain to George that her ex-boyfriend, Mitch, is back on the streets again. George, on the other hand, is laying on his side the bed now, contemplating on if he should tell Miranda where he was today or, just leave it alone since he's handled it himself already. Both parties has their backs toward one another in bed tonight, separated by that dreadful line in the sand, that's forming itself in between their marriage in a way that it never has before. In the past, when they were just boyfriend and girlfriend, Miranda and George would tell each other everything, regardless of how good or bad it may have been. Things have changed now, what was once an open conversation type of couple, has now evolved into a secret keeping married couple, where both parties have decided to keep certain important details to themselves, leaving the other person in complete darkness about what's occurring.

This newly formed routine has continued on for the past few weeks now and tonight is no different. It's to the point now where, some nights, George and Miranda don't even sleep in the same room, in the same bed anymore.

George might fall asleep on the living room's sofa sometimes, while watching a movie or, playing the boys video game. In the past, Miranda would wake George up so he can come in the bedroom with her, where he belongs. These days, she's doing the complete opposite. When George falls asleep in the living room, Miranda doesn't even bother to wake him up to come in the room with her; not because she's asleep herself and doesn't realize that he's not beside her, it's more so as if she could care less now. The weekends are no different. Whenever Miranda's mom would watch Kendal and Kevin sometimes, mostly on the weekends, giving George and Miranda a chance to do things they'd like to do as a couple, they'd jump right on this rare opportunity. Tonight is one of those nights that prove that this theory has drastically changed as well from how it was before. Miranda's home at the present time, Kendal and Kevin are at her mom's house, but, George has decided to spend time with the fellas tonight, which is perfectly fine, every couple needs their space. Only problem is, George hasn't made Miranda aware of where he is this evening.

Miranda's so used to George communicating with her, explaining what he'll be doing and what time she should expect him to arrive back home whenever he goes out. So quite naturally, it's a very odd feeling for Miranda, experiencing something she's not accustomed to. However, Miranda recalls this feeling from past relationships, making it extremely difficult for her to trust the person she's with. So, the first thing that comes to mind for Miranda is, George has to be cheating on her. She doesn't want to accept this whatsoever, but, sitting here all alone tonight, is enabling her to paint a picture in her head about George giving his time, love and affection to another woman, even if this isn't the case. George may be completely innocent in this scenario, just out having fun with the guys to relieve some stress.

Regardless if he is or not, Miranda's mind is made up already about what's taking place with George. Her past has damaged her so severely; mentally, physically and emotionally, Miranda's thoroughly questioning George's true intentions and faithfulness to her.

"It's getting late, fellas," George drunkenly replies, talking in a slurred tone, as he's placing his empty beer bottle in the trash, "I need one of you to give me a lift home if you don't mind."

"Bring your drunken ass on," George's friend, Melvin laughs, as he's reaching in his pocket in search of his car keys, "I'm heading in your direction anyway."

A block away from his house, still in the passenger's seat of Melvin's Ford Pickup truck, George bunglingly drops his cell phone on the floor.

"Damn, I didn't even know that Miranda called me," says George, attempting to adjust his blurry vision on the bright light of his cell phone's screen.

"Well, you better hurry up and get in there before she whoops your ass for being out so late tonight," Melvin chuckles, pulling closely to the curb in front of George's house, "I'll wait here until you get in the house before I pull off though."

Stumbling up the six steps that leads to the front door of his house; George lifelessly flings his hand in the air, signaling to Melvin that he's ok now. Realizing that his buddy has opened the door to get in, Melvin pulls off and heads home himself.

Humming a particular song to himself that played several times at the pool hall tonight, George is placing his keys on the dining room's table, gradually heading into the bedroom to get some much needed rest. George's appetite is consumed tonight, due to the amount of alcohol he digested earlier this evening, so, looking in the microwave to see what Miranda cooked for dinner is pointless.

"Damn, I have to piss bad as shit," George mumbles within, pulling his penis out in the hallway, holding it with his left hand, as he's using the other hand to open the bathroom's door, "Yeah man, this is a relief!"

Shaking the remaining drops of urine from his penis, making sure he doesn't get any on the toilet seat, a discombobulated look has surfaced on George's face, as if he hears something but, is uncertain where the moaning sounds are coming from.

"They're at it again," George whispers, referring to his next door neighbors, Shawn and Tonya, who are known for being vocally disturbing during their sexual encounters in their house at night, "These walls are too thin for them to be making all that damn noise while they're fucking."

To his surprise, when George opened his bedroom's door a minute ago, it was almost as if time stood still for that particular moment in time. Regardless of any noises that were being made by Shawn and Tonya next door, or anyone else for that matter, the only thing George hears right now is complete silence. Whenever any human being is completely stunned or shocked, it does one of two things to them; either causes an instant panic, or, leaves them completely numb, almost to the point that they're actually frozen in place.

In George's case, even though he's a drunken sailor tonight, opening the door to his bedroom, witnessing Miranda fucking another man in their bed, has sobered him up in a heartbeat, but, has also frozen him in place all at the same time. This is a woman that George has been with for years. Miranda was at her breaking point when George first met her, almost as if she had nothing else to live for outside of her two sons. George accepted Miranda's sons, Kendal and Kevin into his life as if he conceived them himself. Despite all of the temptations that life has thrown in his face, even the incident that occurred at his daughter's mother house, when Gina came onto him, George never did anything under the sun to violate or disrespect the mutual bonding between him and his wife, Miranda. His heart is devastated tonight, his foundation has been rocked in a manner that it never has before. How could a woman that he gave his heart, mind, body and trust to, betray him like this.

"Oh my goodness," I'm so sorry, George, "Miranda immediately panics, jumping up out of the bed, not knowing how George will react to her deceitfulness, "I truly am sorry!"

While this untimely incident continues on within Miranda and George's drama-filled bedroom, Miranda's mom, Cathy, isn't feeling well tonight, so, she's bringing Kendal and Kevin home earlier than planned, before heading to the Emergency Room to see what's wrong with her. Cathy tried calling several times earlier to let her daughter know that she was bringing the boys back home tonight instead of tomorrow, but, since she didn't get an answer each time she's called, she's just bringing them to Miranda and George's house anyway.

Cathy was given a spare key by Miranda years ago, in case something went wrong and she needed to get in. Since ringing the doorbell doesn't seem to be issuing any positive results of receiving an answer just like her phone calls didn't, Cathy is using the spare key she has to let herself and the boys in.

"Oh, my," Cathy replies, using her left hand to block Kendal and Kevin's clear pathway of running freely throughout the house, until she finds out what's going on, "You boys stay right here, it sounds like someone is arguing."

Not getting a chance to go find out on her own, the cause of all of this commotion going on in Miranda and George's house, the underlining cause is openly being presented to Cathy, as all three parties in this case are making their way into the living room area.

"Miranda, what's going on in here?" says Cathy, noticing her daughter crying endlessly, standing in the middle of her infuriated husband, George, and her ex-boyfriend, Kendal and Kevin's father, Mitch, trying to prevent them from fighting each other.

After experiencing this gut wrenching ordeal last month, George immediately filed for divorce. Some people seek counseling when things like this occurs within their relationships/marriages but, George is aware of the source of the problem within this marriage and no counselor can tell him differently. Due to the tight bond that was generated over the years between George and Miranda's sons, George still remains in contact with them very often. Mitch, eventually went back to jail two weeks ago and, as of now, Miranda's all alone again, begging George for another chance.

Sarah & Rodney
~ *Discreet Affairs with A Co-Worker* ~

The workplace; for some, is considered as an economical generating safe-haven, a platform strictly used by the working class, providing them with a legitimate way to earn a decent living, or, at least enough to be able to afford the responsibilities that comes along with being an adult.

While this purpose remains true in most cases, for others, they use this worldwide platform as a way to make a living, but also, as their golden opportunity to transform from the conservative person they are at home with their significant other, to the flirtatious type that loves the attention and loves to mingle with anyone of the opposite sex that's showing the slightest bit of interests in them. Let's take a close look at how this plays out between Sarah and Rodney; co-workers that are already involved with someone else.

"Say, sweetie," Sarah replies, blow drying her long, wavy, dark brown-colored hair, as she's looking at Rodney through the mirror that's mounted on their bedroom's wall, "Do you think you'll be off of work in time enough today to put those clothes that's lying over there on the ironing board, in the cleaners that's around the corner from your job?"

"Yeah, I should be able to," Rodney replies, holding his Newport cigarette firmly between the opening of his lips, using both hands to tie the strings of his wheat-colored Timberland boots.

"Thanks, boo, you're so good to me," Sarah smiles, rocking back and forth to the melody that's flowing from the stereo system in the living room, "Give mommy some sugah before you leave out for work."

Poking her full-sized lips out, anxiously anticipating a passionate kiss from Rodney, Sarah momentarily flinches when she opens her eyes to realize which set of lips Rodney's aiming for.

"Get up from down there, boy," Sara laughs out loud, "Keep it up and you're going to get some shit started, preventing you from going to work today!"

Rising up off of his knees, in a standing position, Rodney grabs his backpack off of the bedroom's door knob, dangling his keys loosely in his hands, as he's heading off to work.

"Shit, I have a slow leak in my fucking back tire again," says Rodney, surveying the area he's parked in for the slightest trace of broken glass or a nail, "I just paid 40 bucks the other day to get a new tire put on the front, now the back tire is losing air."

Popping the trunk of his navy blue-colored Nissan Maxima, Rodney's reaching down inside the trunk in search of his electrical air-pump. Carefully placing Sarah's clothes in the back seat of his car, that needs to be dropped off at the Cleaners; Rodney's forcefully pressing the cord of the air-pump down into the cigarette lighter of his car, flicking the switch on it to see if it's powered up.

"I know I'm going to be late as shit today as slow as this thing pumps out air," Rodney assumes, taking turns of glancing down at the amount of air that's being pumped into his tire, to observing the time on his Stainless Steel watch.

Rodney has been on the losing end of random, sporadic problems lately and, the lead supervisor at his job, Mr. Thomas, already made Rodney aware that, if he doesn't change his pattern of being tardy so frequently and/or calling out so often, he'd have to relieve Rodney of his duties as one of the top employees at Inner City Advertising Company. Rodney has been on this job for a little over 5 years now and truthfully speaking, he doesn't see himself doing anything else; legally anyway. On this particular day, a slight bit of lady luck has finally made her presence known to Rodney, abruptly erasing a tiny portion of the misfortune he's been on the receiving end of recently.

A young lady by the name of, Chassidy Moore, is being trained today to fill one of the available positions as a Salesperson, causing Mr. Thomas' attention to be solely on her at the moment, not realizing that Rodney just arrived to work, a half hour late.

"About time your ass showed up," Rodney's co-worker, Bruce playfully replies, walking over to shake Rodney's hand, "As you can see, we have some fresh meat on the team."

Looking around at each desk in search of the fresh meat that Bruce is referring to, Rodney is immediately in awe when his eyes make contact with Chassidy's eyes.

"Aw, damn," Rodney mumbles, titling his head to the side to get a glimpse of Chassidy's legs that are hidden beneath her desk, "Did she just start working here today, Bruce?"

"See, if you reported to work every day as scheduled, you wouldn't have to ask questions like that one," Bruce laughs, "But, to answer your question, yes, this is Mrs. Moore's first day on the job. Not that it should matter to you though, Mr. Romeo, she's married and you're involved already."

"Ah, whatever, player hater," Rodney replies, pulling out the chair to his desk, which is diagonally positioned across from where Chassidy's seated, "I didn't say I was going to try anything with her, I was just asking if today was her first day here at work, that's all."

"Yeah, right," Bruce smiles, not believing one word that's coming out of Rodney's mouth.

The afternoon has arrived now and after watching Chassidy all morning, Rodney's about to make his first move by formerly introducing himself to her.

"Say, Miss," Rodney begins, leaning forward across his desk to get Chassidy's attention, "I know today is your first day working here and all but, how do you like it so far?"

"Ah, it's not so bad," Chassidy shrugs her shoulders, money green-colored eyes mesmerizing Rodney to the fullest, as she's giving him eye-to-eye contact with each response, "It beats the job at Macy's that I had prior to this job."

"Yeah, I know that's right," Rodney chuckles, laughing at a comment that wasn't even funny, trying to get on Chassidy's good side right away, "I know it's none of my business, but, do you live in this area?"

"You're right, it's not," Chassidy politely grins after her splurge remark, "But, I will say, I don't live too far from here."

Noticing the diamond-cut wedding ring that Chassidy's proudly wearing, that's radiantly sparkling each time the sunlight reflects off of it, Rodney progressively follows up with his next comment,

"Whoever your husband is, he's a lucky ass man to have a woman as sexy as you are."

Chassidy is a voluptuous woman, with a curvaceous body of a goddess. Any man who crosses her path will immediately experience an initial reaction to her physical appearance. Not only is Chassidy beautiful beyond words, her mannerism and intellect solidifies her stature above most women. Some men are easily intimidated; others have the boldness it takes to approach a woman of her caliber, just not the swagger she finds attractive in a man. So, at this point, everything that Rodney's saying to Chassidy at the moment, sounds like a broken record; she's heard it over and over again from different men who's trying to steal some of her husband's glory of having her on their arm. In Chassidy's eyes, Rodney's no different from any other man who has come onto her in the past. For all she know, he's probably involved himself already, but is quite naturally saying all of the things he thinks a woman wants to hear, in an attempt of wooing her out of her panties. Unfortunately for Rodney, Chassidy's highly experienced with different aspects of life and, is currently showing no signs of interest in him.

"It's nice fraternizing with you today, Rodney," Chassidy softly replies, sliding her medicated glasses back on her eyes, as she's focusing on her computer screen again, "However, it's time for me to get back to work now."

Presently stunned at the fact that none of his top lines that usually seals the deal for him when attempting to reel in a woman, had no effect whatsoever on Chassidy today, Rodney's fidgety tapping his pencil on his desk, as his mind searches for the proper techniques it takes to win over a woman like Chassidy.

The silver lining in this whole ordeal seemingly benefits the Inner-City Advertising Company more than it does for anyone else. Hiring Chassidy turns out to be one of the wisest business decisions this company's made in years. Chassidy's expertise in the sales department, combined with her professional business oriented mentality, has new clientele coming in weekly. Chassidy's presence within this company is also causing Rodney to show up to work every day, on time at that, as scheduled. Not everyone is a profitable winner in this scenario though. With everything in life, in order to keep the balance of good versus evil on-going, wherever there's any positivity or goodness taking place, evil and/or negativity isn't too far behind.

"Ah, Chassidy," Chassidy's husband, Bill yells out from the bedroom area, "Fix me a turkey and cheese sandwich and bring it in when you come, if you don't mind, sweetheart."

"Sure thing, dear," Chassidy loudly replies, "Would you like something to drink with your sandwich as well?"

"A cold soda will do, honey," Bill reciprocates.

When Chassidy married Bill seven years ago, she literally married herself right into a rich family. When Bill's father passed away last summer, he left Bill a huge lump sum of money and sole ownership of a few lucrative businesses that he owned. Chassidy was fully aware of the amount of fortune the Moore family possessed and, having Bill as her lawfully wedded husband, entitled her to a decent portion of their wealth. However, for whatever reasons, Bill always made Chassidy work somewhere, regardless of the amount of money and wealth 'HE' acquired.

Even though Chassidy enjoys using the natural assets God's blessed her with physically, to attract as much attention as she can from guys, toying with their emotions and imaginations, she'll never go so far as to lose everything she has in Bill. If she ever decides to see someone else on the side, it'll always be limited; she'll never allow things to get too deep with that person. Now on the other hand, Rodney doesn't give a fuck one way or another. If things don't work out between him and Sarah, so be it, he'll just move on to the next one. Sarah doesn't feel this way though. Her feelings toward Rodney are the complete opposite. During the course of their relationship, Rodney has done his fair share of heartbreaking, but apparently, not enough to make Sarah leave.

Sarah has been in a few knockdown, drag out type of fights with different women and all of those beefs stemmed from Rodney's infidelities. Like always though, whenever Sarah's upset with Rodney, no matter how pissed off she may be, Rodney always does little slick shit sexually, to make her love him even more.

"Babe, I think we should go to the movies tonight," Sarah suggests, quietly walking up behind Rodney in the bathroom, leaning her head against his bare back while he's trimming his mustache and side burns, "We haven't been out in awhile and I want to see the new Harry Potter flick while it's playing."

"Harry Potter," Rodney mutters, curling his top lip down, making sure he's precisely lining it up correctly, "I thought you was going to say some shit like, Tyler Perry or, Ice Cube's movie. You want to see Harry Potter though!"

"What, it's nothing wrong with Harry Potter movies, babe," Sarah exclaims, running her soft hand gracefully up Rodney's muscular cut abs, "It's breaking records worldwide with the sales it's generating and, I guess you'd have to be sophisticated minded person to enjoy a movie like that."

"I'm just not into that type of shit, Sarah, sophisticated or not, but, if you want to see it, I'll roll with you."

"Ok, babe, I'll go get dressed!" Sarah gleefully replies.

Evening time has arrived and, after getting dressed, standing in a long line for tickets, popcorn and sodas, Rodney and Sarah are making their way to their seats.

"It's two empty seats over there," Sara points, excusing herself, as her and Rodney are squeezing their way through the crowded isles.

"I hope this shit isn't as long as that movie, Titantic was back in the day," says Rodney, comfortably positioning himself in his seat, as he's already reaching into the tall tube of butter-flavored popcorn, "If so, I'm falling asleep on you, Sarah, straight up."

Falling asleep is the last thing Rodney's doing though. True, this movie is extremely long, but, it just dawned on Rodney that he discreetly overlooked Chassidy's files at work today with her number on it, so, instead of calling, he's trying his hand at sending a text to see if he'll get a response. Rodney's cell phone's ringer is off right now, making it extremely impossible for Sarah to pick up on what he's discreetly doing in this pitch-dark movie theatre.

Once the text message has been successfully sent to Chassidy's phone and she finds out that it's Rodney sending it, she can either ignore the texts or, participate by responding to what's being sent to her.

Holding his thumb over the red light indicator of his cell phone that informs him that a new voicemail or text has been sent, Rodney's slowly removing his thumb, peeping down to see if the right light is appearing. At first, nothing appeared at all. The only thing Rodney sees is the BlackBerry logo embedded on the top part of his screen and, the Sprint logo all the way at the bottom. Outside of that, the only light that's flashing before Rodney's eyes is the lights from the movie screen. Frustrated that this tactic doesn't appear to be working at the moment either, Rodney's leaning his head back against his seat, hoping this movie is almost over with.

After realizing that he still has another hour to go, Rodney's slipping his hand into his pocket once again, this time easing his cell phone out to see the red light indicator blinking off and on. Rodney's heart is thumping with joy right now but, he doesn't want to become too excited. Rodney still doesn't know if this is Chassidy responding and, if so, he doesn't know what type of response she's sent. Flickering his curious finger across any button on the phone that'll cause the blank screen to light up, Rodney is pleased that he's made it pass the first step of this dueling texting approach, realizing that the response was sent by Chassidy, as she's questioning who this is that's texting her.

Urgently typing up a response to catch Chassidy while he can, Rodney's briefly startled when Sarah looks over at him and replies,

"Rodney, who are you texting?"

Without any time to think of rapid comeback for this question, Rodney's blurting out the first name that comes to mind,

"Oh, that's just Steve texting to ask me if I'm watching the basketball game tonight."

"Well, stop texting Steve," Sarah annoyingly whispers, "This is our time together, Rodney, and it's highly rude of you to be texting him on our night out with each other."

"Cool, shortie, I won't text him back," Rodney replies, glancing down at his phone, realizing that Chassidy responded back again.

Eagerly anxious to arrive home to check his text message and respond to Chassidy, Rodney immediately rushes into the bathroom after arriving home, knowing that this is one of the only rooms in the house that he can get a brief break to himself. For the past half hour, Rodney has been texting away on his phone, which means Chassidy is obviously responding. Sarah has knocked on the bathroom's door three times already, asking Rodney what's taking him so long to come out, just to receive the lame excuse that his stomach is bothering him. Honestly speaking, the only thing that's causing Rodney to exit the bathroom now is, Chassidy has subsequently ended the texts on her behalf for the evening.

Today is Friday and, Rodney can't wait to get to work to see what sexy assemble Chassidy's wearing today. Chassidy's attire usually consists of an extravagant combination, Mondays through Thursdays; of something sexy but, on the casual side at the same time. Now on Fridays, Chassidy has appointed this day as her 'Head Boggling' day of the week. Damn near every Friday, Chassidy usually turns things up a notch, showing plenty of cleavage with her V-neck shirts or, leaving at least three of the buttons at the top of her blouse unbuttoned for everyone to see her breasts stuffed in her bra. To top things off, all the guys at the office receives a birds-eye-view of seeing that entire ass crammed in her tight mini-skirts that are also worn by Chassidy on Fridays.

Slowly but surely, as days turned into weeks, weeks turned into months, Chassidy voluntarily began to open up more to Rodney. Outside of their discreet dinner dates, they both came to a mutual agreement of the respectful times they are to communicate with one another outside of the work place. Chassidy has made Rodney fully aware of Bill's work schedule, enabling him to be precise with the times of the day he decides to text or call. Meanwhile, by Rodney's girlfriend, Sarah only working part-time right now, Rodney has also made Chassidy aware that he can only promptly respond during the daytime hours, anytime before 5:00. After five, Sarah's usually in his presence, making it hard for Rodney to have a continuous text session with anyone, unless he isolates himself in a secluded area of the house to do so. When this unfaithful act all began not too long ago, Chassidy did slip up a time or two, texting Rodney beyond the midnight hour. This brief 'accident' undoubtedly led to a ferocious argument between Sarah and Rodney that night when Rodney forgot to turn the ringer of his cell phone off and Sarah heard it.

Like always, Sarah considered that incident to be water under the bridge as well, deciding to continue on clinging to her deceitful boyfriend's arm, feeling as though she can't do any better than what Rodney's dishing out to her. However, what I witnessed with my very own eyes today, informs me without any doubts that, Sarah has finally reached her boiling point and trust me when I tell you, it wasn't pretty.

The thing that most likely fucked it all up for Rodney was using someone's name, his friend, Kenny, as his alibi, the person he was supposedly hanging out with last night. Unfortunately, he must have forgotten two things. One, Sarah knows mostly all of his friends and has their phone numbers and two; he didn't make Kenny aware of what he was doing so Kenny could cover for him.

As a result, Kenny called Rodney's house looking for him last night after Rodney flat out told Sarah this morning when he got home that, he'd been out with Kenny all night and crashed at his place because he was too drunk to drive home. By Kenny calling, it immediately blew Rodney's cover, revealing that this wasn't the person Rodney was with all night last night. Rodney is unaware that Kenny has even called though. He got up this morning, got dressed, kissed Sarah on the cheek and headed off to work as if everything is covered.

This Tuesday morning is completely different from any other Tuesday when it comes to the systematic routine of Sarah and Rodney. Sarah's discreetly disguised in Sandy's car, one of her closest girlfriend's, parked right outside of Rodney's job, waiting patiently to witness who Rodney comes out with. Now, if Rodney would've just said goodbye to Chassidy, simply ending their work day in that manner, he'd still be somewhat on easy streak, but, this wasn't the case. Chassidy requested a kiss before departing with Rodney and that's exactly what she received, causing Rodney to receive the thrusting end of a rock hard, aluminum baseball bat when Sarah saw him, jumped out of Sandy's car and initiated her attack. With all of the turmoil taking place out here, right where I'm standing at now, caused the police to arrive on the scene in a matter of minutes, earlier today.

Chassidy hopped in her car and fled away from the scene the moment she saw Sarah approaching Rodney. Ever since that day, she hasn't reported to work at all. Rodney, however, was released from the hospital this evening, returning home to a house that I'm not sure if Sarah still resides in or not. I do know that Sarah wasn't arrested tonight because I saw her get back in the car with Sandy. Where they went after leaving here beats me.

Interlude
~ Playing the Game- As the Dealer & As the Receiver ~

From a personal standpoint, a male's point of view, the desolation concept of cheating, eventually concludes in chaos for all parties involved. Summarizing this concept all up for you, in this case, I'll paint a picture in your minds of a card game being played under the bright, exciting city lights of sin city, Las Vegas, Nevada. Picture in your minds sitting at a colorful card game table, the stakes are detrimentally high, the loud sounds around you of ringing slot machines, overly excited jackpot winners screaming at the top of their lungs and loose change jiggling back and forth in a nervous person's hand, hoping that the last few tokens they're sliding into the slot machines, will somehow triple its value for them, is distracting your concentration way beyond belief.

The 'DEALER' is synonymous to the cheating person in the relationship. He takes pride in dishing out all types of hands and tricky situations because, in all actuality at this point, he stands nothing to lose. In the midst of dealing several hands out to you, he gets to sit back and observe the multiple amounts of expressions written on your faces, as you're attempting to adapt and adjust yourself to the cards you've been dealt. Most times, you're fully aware that you're in a 'no win' situation; the cards you've been dealt has no possibilities of making you come out on the winning end. This entire card game is designed with the intentions of benefitting the house, the place the game is being played, in any and every way imaginable.

The same applies to a relationship when you're being cheated on. The 'Dealer', the person that's cheating on you, is taking a huge risk by doing so, but, he/she is enjoying every bit of taking this uncalled for risk to the point that, it continues on for as long as they see that they're actually getting away with it. They are fully aware of your ways by now, your daily routine, likes and dislikes, so, they know exactly what buttons to push and the exact time to push them, toying with you as if you're a robot being controlled by the mash of a button.

Truth be told, even after finding out what's being done to them, some people still choose to remain in the relationship/marriage, feeling as though they can't do any better and/or, using the kids as an excuse for them to remain with someone whose love has obviously taken its course with them. When things have escalated to the heights of this level, the 'Dealer', is in a 'win-win' situation at this point. To use an old cliché, he/she gets to have their cake and eat it too when; they've made their partner in the relationship/marriage fully aware that, they're seeing other people outside of them, but, the person being told this in the relationship/marriage, decides to remain in it anyway.

The ones who decide to tolerate this behavior, in some point in their lives, have experienced a low self-esteem complex, sometimes stemming from something that occurred within their childhood, or, criticism from a family member, abused in a relationship, etc. Everyone wants to be loved, accepted and appreciated but, when this isn't being received, some settle for whatever is being presented to them that at least comes slightly close to what they're seeking in a companion.

Now, from my own personal circumstances I've dealt with in life, I can honestly share these lessons with you open heartedly, being completely truthful from beginning to end. While reading this book, some of you might be able to identify with a few things I've said, some might be able to identify with one of the characters I've used in one of the four stories or, some might be able to identify with this entire book, word for word. So you'll know, even though I used fictional characters names in these stories, the stories themselves are all 'Based On True Stories' that I've either witnessed with my very own eyes, experienced myself or, have heard about at some point in my everyday daily life. To protect the identity of these people who've actually experienced these dreadful circumstances, I decided to respectfully use fictional characters names.

Moving along, now that I've described what the 'Dealer's' task consist of, the one who's cheating in the relationship, I'm going to elaborate now on the 'Receiver', the one who's being cheated on.

   The 'RECEIVER', the one being cheated on in the relationship/marriage, is always considered as the vulnerable party in this equation. Most times, they're doing their best in the relationship/marriage, attempting to be loved in the same fashion that they're dishing the love out. Offers are presented to them on different occasions; tempting their true aspects of remaining faithful to the person they're involved with. If this person genuinely loves the person they're involved with, with no questions asked, they'll reject these offers every time they're confronted with them, choosing to remain loyal and faithful to the person they're involved with. The 'Receiver', the one being cheated on, is also often times accused by the 'Dealer', as being the one who's cheating. You see, when indulging in the discretion act of cheating, reverse psychology is often exercised.

The 'Dealer', often times attempts to overwhelm the 'Receiver', the one being cheated on, with a suffocating amount of guilt, as if they're the ones presenting the problem within the relationship/marriage. If allowed, this procedure will steal any amount of positive energy that the 'Receiver' has left within themselves, depressing them with enough negative energy that'll eventually lead to them questioning themselves about what they're doing wrong and, what they can be doing better. After successfully making the 'Receiver' feel this way, the 'Dealer' converts right back to what he/she was doing at first, being unfaithful.

From the first two stories I've shared with you so far, I want to highlight a few key factors from each story, that are red flag signs of a person that's being unfaithful and how you can detect it within your own relationships/ marriages. First, I'll elaborate on George and Miranda's situation. Often times these days, I'll run across different women claiming that it's no good men in the world today. Reason being, they've constantly aligned themselves with men who've dogged them out, making them feel completely useless during the relationships. As a result, some women have even gone so far as to seeking the love and affection that's been eluding them when it comes to the men they've dealt with, to looking for it in another woman.

In Miranda's case, even though her ex-boyfriend, Mitch, Kendal and Kevin's father, put her through pure hell when they were together, as an end result, she still chose to deal with Mitch sexually, even though she had a loving husband in George. George is the type of guy that I hear some women claiming isn't out here in the world today. He's a hard working man, a loving family man, respectful, honest and loyal to the woman he's with, but, as a reward for being such a gentlemen, he's undeniably betrayed by the woman who supposedly loves him the most, his wife, Miranda; the same person looking for a 'good man.'

To make matters worse, Kendal and Kevin has to suffer as well because, they've actually grown to know and accept George as the positive male role model in their lives, when their biological father was nowhere to be found. Now, they're stuck dead in the middle of the drama their mother has caused, leaving them with the tough decision of potentially having to break their bond they've created with George.

For me, observing these two constantly trying to come to grips with the trials and tribulations that life poured into their marriage, often times had me in the position as the advice giver. I know both of them extremely well and, on a regular basis, George would call me sometimes explaining what he's going through and, I'm assuming whenever Miranda wasn't confining in one of her girlfriends for advice, is when she'd call to talk with me as well. I can honestly vouch for George that he's a good man. Even though he's going through hell with his spiteful daughter's mom, Gina, trying to earn enough money to pay off the back child support he owes so he can obtain his Driver's License again, George still insists on pushing forward. When most men would've broken under pressure, voluntarily giving into the temptations of being sexually intimate with a woman outside of the relationship/marriage, George rejected the offer to do so with his daughter's mom. The red flags of something shaky occurring in this marriage were all on Miranda's behalf.

First, take a good look at the phone situation. Whenever George entered the house and/or room that Miranda was in, she'd hang up the phone, claiming that it was a relative she was conversing with. If this is so, what's wrong with her talking to her relative while George is in her presence? Also, if you noticed, it was never a family outing occurring in this marriage. If anything, George was the one spending quality time with Miranda's sons, Kevin and Kendal, while Miranda was always home by herself, doing God knows what.

What amazes me the most is, I've witnessed these two getting along perfectly fine, family outings and all, when they were in a relationship. Somehow, which is still a mystery to me, not only with Miranda and George but, with other couples as well is how drastically things can change after these couples become husband and wife. The relationships seemingly last forever but, as soon as they decide to tie the knot, the marriages take a turn for the worse, in no time!

Sarah and Rodney's situation is something else as well. It's a known fact that, some affairs take place right within the workplace. If the attraction is there with someone on the job and something isn't being fulfilled at home, the work place becomes a sinful sanctuary that's used for discreetly cheating and having these unfulfilled desires handled. The one who's having the affair, flirting, or, has a crush on a co-worker, feels as though they'll never be exposed for doing so; at least not any time soon. They can use the job as an excuse any time they see fit. Sometimes, they'll claim to be working overtime or, maybe their job is supposedly having a party, depending on the holiday season and/or special occasion. Also, their selective choice of clothing that they wear to work tells a lot about them as well. For a woman, she'll revert to wearing tight clothing, giving a slight tease of her breasts and/or legs and thighs, only if no dress code is in place at the job she works at. In most cases, this is obviously done to attract attention and, it should be a red flag for her boyfriend/husband, if he's observing it. A guy doesn't really resort to this type of tactic when he's being unfaithful with someone at the workplace. Most times, he might groom himself a little better, switching cologne, carrying extra clothing to work with him and often times more concerned about his body, suggesting that he needs to work-out more.

Texting also plays a huge role in these scenarios as well. With the diverse amount of high-tech technology we use daily these days for communication, the concept of texting ranks at the very top of this list. Rodney resorted to it in the movie theatre that night, texting his co-worker, Chassidy, even while he was sitting beside his girlfriend, Sarah. Sarah would never know who he's communicating with, unless she violates his privacy by snatching his cell phone or, discreetly roaming through it whenever Rodney is asleep, which some people seriously reverts to doing.

To break-a-way from their observing companions who might have an inkling that something is going on, some people isolate themselves in a private room of the house; bathroom, basement, attic, etc., giving them some free time alone to respond through texts to the person they're cheating with. In most cases, a communicating schedule has been developed and agreed upon by the parties who are being unfaithful. They make each other aware of a decent time to call and/or text, making sure the person that they're involved with in the relationship/marriage, doesn't begin to suspect anything. Every now and then, this agreed upon time schedule is violated by someone though. An unexpected text or call will randomly occur during the night, causing an immediate altercation within the relationship/marriage, if the cheating party doesn't promptly come up with a reasonable explanation, that's believed, of why someone else is calling and/or texting so late at night.

Don't get it mistaken though, everyone that texts, isn't necessarily cheating. You'd have to study your companions' daily behavior patterns to see if any legitimate red flag signs are presenting themselves. But I will say; if you have a gut feeling that you're being cheated on, most times, you are. At this point, you've obviously revealed something within your companion that's causing this feeling.

To summarize things up, pertaining to Sarah and Rodney, Rodney had no clue that Sarah had a plan up her sleeve of how to catch him in the act of being unfaithful. Sarah went so far as to show up at the workplace, discreetly hiding herself outside in her friend's car, Sandy, until this heart-wrenching circumstance literally presented itself right before her very eyes of Rodney being unfaithful and, who he was being unfaithful with. Its cases like this one, that often times lead to someone getting seriously hurt, if not killed. Lucky enough for Rodney, Sarah's assault on him with the baseball bat she used, didn't result in his fatality.

Now, let's continue on with the last two stories of this book and, pay close attention to how these unfaithful incidents unfold.

Monica & Devin
~ Is Blood Really Thicker Than Water ~

This unpredictable world that we live in can often times back us into a corner on several occasions, lashing out an unforgiving test of our faith, when things aren't going so well with us, financially, mentally, physically and socially. While some people in this world takes pride and honor in lending a helping hand to someone that's going through rough times in their lives, not for bragging rights but, because it's the humanitarian thing to do, others look down their noses as if they're high and mighty, not wanting to be bothered at all, even if they are in a position to help. When going through tough times in life and, you've basically exhausted all of your avenues of getting back on track on your own, family members will most likely be your next alternative of where your support system will arise from. But, what if your family members betray you as well, turning their backs on you faster than a stranger on the streets would, what do you do then?

"Man, that weekend get-a-way to the Bahamas was so romantic, boo," Monica replies, unpacking her luggage bags, as she's storing her clothes away in the walk-in closet of the bedroom, "I think we need to seriously consider doing this more often."

"Ha, that's easier said than done," Devin chuckles, flopping down on their king-sized bed, as if he hasn't slept in days.

"Well, my mom volunteered to watch Lil' Devin for us whenever we needed her to, so, what's the problem?"

"Baby, you know I just recently received a promotion at my job the other day," Devin explains, sliding his hands behind his head on the pillow, as he's glancing over at Monica, "Hell, I almost wasn't able to get time off this weekend in order for us to go to the Bahamas. Mills Tire & Lube Company will literally fall apart if I'm not present to keep business flowing sufficiently."

"Fall apart if you're not there," Monica frowns, "What in the hell is Justin's purpose of showing up at that job if you're talking like you're the boss yourself?"

"No, Justin is the boss, babe, I'm just saying . . ."

"Hold that thought for a sec," Monica intervenes, rushing over to answer the telephone before it stops ringing, "Hello."

"Monica, it happened again," her cousin, Christian replies, crying hysterical on the phone, "I promised myself that I'd never allow him to put his hands on me again, but, he did, just a few minutes ago."

"Oh, no," Monica panics, clenching her chest tightly, as she's listening to the pain and nervousness in her cousin's voice, "Did you at least call the police on his ass, Christian?"

"Babe, what's wrong?" Devin quietly whispers, noticing a troubled look written on Monica's face.

"Hold up baby," says Monica, holding her left hand over the mouthpiece of the phone, as she turns to whisper at Devin, "I'll tell you when I hang up from my cousin."

"I'm just fed up with this shit, Monica," Christian wearisomely replies, "I want out of this abusive ass relationship but, I honestly have nowhere else to live."

"Yes you do, Christian," Monica replies, without discussing things with Devin first, "Pack up whatever belongings you have and bring them with you over here. We have a guest room that's not being occupied and you can stay in there until you find a place of your own."

"Say, babe, why did you tell her that?" Devin frustratingly replies, rising up in a sitting position on the bed, momentarily tuning out the basketball game that he's watching.

"She's my blood, Devin," Monica quietly responds, giving Devin a harsh look, as if she wishes he would wait until she hangs up the phone to ask questions, "What else do you expect for me to do?"

Shaking his head; completely disappointed that Monica didn't run this sporadic decision by him first before inviting Christian to stay with them, Devin snatches a pillow and blanket out of the bedroom's closet and proceeds into the living room.

"Ugh, he's so fucking immature," Monica blurts out, storming into the living room area behind Devin, after hanging up the phone with Christian, "Is my cousin staying here with us for a few days, going to kill you, Devin?"

"A few days," Devin urgently replies, becoming highly agitated with each word that's coming out of Monica's mouth, "You just told her that she can stay here until she finds a place of her own, Monica. You think that shit is only going to take a few days as hard as times are economically these days!"

"You're fucking unbelievable," says Monica, anxiously pacing back and forth from the dining room to the kitchen, "My damn cousin calls, explaining to me that she just been physically abused by her boyfriend, Mike, and you expect me to just leave her high and dry, without at least coming to her aid of inviting her to stay here?"

"You know what, Monica," Devin sternly replies, "Do whatever the hell you want with your cousin and anyone else from your family. None of them has respectfully accepted me ever since you and I have been together anyway and all of a sudden, you think I'm supposed to be joyful about you inviting any of them over here!"

"You're a damn lie, Devin, and you know it. My family does accept you."

"Monica, seriously though, you can go ahead with that bullshit. Before that phone call a minute ago, everything was going perfectly normal between us. Hell, we just got back home from our weekend vacation. Just like that, you had to open your big ass mouth, volunteering our house as the resting place for another guest."

"Like I said before, Devin, she's my blood and I refuse to leave her out in the dark regardless of the smart ass comments you decide to say about it."

"Fine, do as you please, Monica, but, you will regret this decision you've made in the future, mark my words."

"Yeah, whatever, nigga," Monica sarcastically replies, as she turns to head back into the bedroom.

Bright and early the next morning, as planned, Christian has began packing the few belongings she has at her place, trying to sneak away before running into her abusive husband again. Although she called the police last night on Mike, after he viciously assaulted her for arriving home so late, Mike had already fled away from the scene before the cops even arrived. True, at this point, Mike does have a warrant out for his arrest but, in the meantime, he's still a free man and has every opened opportunity of eventually crossing paths with Christian again. Nevertheless, as she's exiting the duplex of her apartment, Christian has spotted Mike again, wandering around across the street from her apartment, right in front of the liquor store.

"Fuck," Christian quietly mutters, nervously dodging back inside of the apartment before Mike notices her, "The damn battery of my cell phone is dead now because I forgot to charge it up last night."

Not having a way to contact Monica now, by her cell phone being dead and, the house phone was disconnected months ago, Christian's balled up in a fetal position on the living room's floor, waiting for her first opening of rushing to her car before Mike approaches her. Right around the corner, about 20 minutes away from where Christian lives, Monica's picking Lil' Devin up from her mom's house.

"Hmmm, I haven't heard from Christian this morning," Monica mumbles within, scrolling through her cell phone in search of Christian's phone number, "Let me call her to make sure everything's ok."

Not getting an answer each time she's calling because of Christian's cell phone going directly to voicemail, Monica's securely fastening Lil' Devin's seatbelt across him in the back seat of her Honda Accord, before heading toward Christian's house.

"Did you enjoy your weekend with your grandma, Lil' Devin?" Monica inquires, glancing in the rear view mirror, as she's anticipating Lil' Devin's response.

"I guess," Lil' Devin replies, giving his WWE action figure more attention than he's giving this conversation with his mom.

"What do you mean you guess, Lil' Devin," says Monica, pulling up in an empty parking spot on Christian's front, "If you don't know if you had fun or not then, who should I ask?"

"It was ok, mom," Lil' Devin annoyingly responds, "I should've taken my video game with me though, so I'd have something else to do other than being bothered with my cousin, Leah, all weekend."

"Ah, Leah wasn't that bad now, was she Lil' Devin?"

"Mom, bad isn't the word."

Hearing the engine of Monica's Honda Accord shutting off, followed by the emergency break being pulled up, Christian's peeping through the mini-blinds in her living, trying to see who car this is on her front.

"Thank you, Lord," Christian's replies with a sigh of relief, realizing that Monica has come to her rescue.

Not getting a chance to get out of her car to ring Christian's doorbell, Monica's immediately approached by Christian, who's suggesting that they hurry up and get in the car and leave the area.

"What's wrong, Christian," Monica's nervously turning the key in the ignition to start up the car; "Mike didn't come back again, did he?"

"Girl, yes," says Christian, surveying the entire area for any signs of Mike, "He was standing outside of that liquor store that's across the street from me this morning, the one located right on the corner."

"This is some crazy shit," Monica quietly utters, not talking too loudly so Lil' Devin can't hear what's being said, "Well, at least he doesn't know where I live so, you should be straight for awhile, Christian."

Meanwhile, on the East-Side of town, Devin's tallying up whatever amount of revenue Mills' Tire & Lube Company generated today, safely securing it in their secret hiding spot.

"I'm gone for today, Devin," says one of the employees, Russell, as he's swiping his time card and proceeding out the door.

"All right, Russell, I'll see you in the morning," Devin stretches and yawns, looking down at his watch to see what time it is.

 Storing everything away in its proper places and setting the alarm system, Devin's turning off all of the lights in the building before heading home himself for the evening. Knowing that it's a strong possibility that his unwanted guest, Christian, has already arrived at his house, Devin's prolonging the process of heading home by stopping at nearest McDonald's first.

"Ah, can I have the number two value meal, no cheese and an Iced-Tea as the drink," Devin loudly replies, leaning his head outside of the driver's side door of his car to speak into the loud speaker.

"Will that be all today, Sir?"

"Yes, that's all," says Devin, gradually pulling around in the drive-thru to receive his food.

Deciding to go on home after leaving McDonald's, to face the unwanted task of having one of Monica's relatives staying with them, Devin arrives home a half hour later to his excited son who's happy to see him.

"Hey, daddy," Lil' Devin excitedly rushes toward his father, "What did you bring me back to eat from McDonald's?"

"You're only happy to see me because of this McDonald's bag I have in my hand, boy?" Devin jokingly replies, walking toward the kitchen to cut his sandwich in half to share with his son.

"Hey, Devin, how have you been?" Christian speaks, exiting the guest room she'll be residing in until she finds a place of her own.

"Hey, Christian," Devin forcefully responds, "I'm hanging in there and yourself?"

"Just thankful that you guys are allowing me to stay here with you for awhile," says Christian.

"Christian," Monica intervenes, cleansing her hands with the hand sanitizer she has on them, "It's some clean towels and wash clothes right here in the hallway's closet, feel free to help yourself to them whenever you need to."

"Ok, cousin, thank you so much for doing this for me," Christian utters, glancing in the hallway's closet at the neatly stacked clothes and towels that Monica has stored away.

"A thank you isn't necessary, Christian," Monica smiles, "I'm sure you'd do the same for me if the shoe was on the other foot."

"Say, Monica," Christian slightly giggles, "I see you're still as neat as you were when we was little girls growing up."

"Oh, yes indeed," Monica smirks, throwing a load of clothes in the washing machine, while she's holding a conversation with Christian, "I can't stand the slightest bit of dirt being in here."

In the other room, tired from another long, stressful day at work, Devin's throwing his trash in the trashcan, before escorting Lil' Devin into the bathroom to bathe him.

"Come on, Lil' squirt," Devin tickles his son, lifting him over his shoulder, as he's racing down the hallway toward the bathroom, "It's time for you to take a bath and brush your teeth before going to bed. We have to get up early in the morning so, let's get a move on."

Later that evening in bed, not much is being said between Devin and Monica. Devin's flipping through the cable channels in search of something to watch while Monica's sitting up, polishing her toe nails.

"How long are we going to do this, Devin?" say Monica.

"How long are we going to do what?" Devin responds.

"This silent treatment, Devin, don't you think this shit is a little juvenile?"

"If you have something to say, Monica, just say it," Devin nonchalantly utters, "You don't seem to have any problem saying what you have to say any other time."

"See what I mean," Monica rolls her eyes, leaning forward to fan her royal blue colored nail polish until it dries on her toe nails, "You always have a smart ass response for everything I ask you."

"I'm not going to argue with you tonight, Monica," says Devin, tossing the remote control aside, turning over on his side until he falls asleep.

"I'm so sick of this shit," Monica mumbles, placing her blindfold over her eyes, as she's adjusting her head on her fluffy pillow.

Morning time in Monica and Devin's house is usually extremely busy. Both are faced with the draining tasks of washing up, getting dressed, getting Lil' Devin prepared and, whenever possible, grabbing a bite to eat before heading off to work. Since Christian's staying here for awhile, Monica feels as though one of their daily tasks of dropping Lil' Devin off at Daycare, or, at her mom's house, has been temporarily eliminated. Christian has volunteered to look out for Lil' Devin so Monica and Devin can go to work.

"Are you sure you can handle him by yourself, Christian?" Monica replies with a concerned look on her face. "Lil' Devin can become very hyper at times."

"Girl, go on to work," says Christian, softly bumping her hip against Monica's leg, "Besides, one good deed deserves another."

"All right, Christian," Monica hesitatingly approaches the front door of her house, "If you have any problems at all, and I mean any problems, call me at my job right away."

"Monica, everything will be fine," Christian insists.

Building up her confidence enough in Christian to give her a chance at watching Lil' Devin, Monica eventually turns the door knob and exits the house, a half hour after Devin has already left out for work.

"Hey, Lil' Devin," Christian replies, holding Lil' Devin's hand, as they're walking toward the kitchen, "Tell Auntie Christian what you'd like to have for breakfast so I can make it for you."

"Just a bowl of Fruity Pebbles," says Lil' Devin, still fidgeting with his WWE action figures that he's holding in his hands.

"I see you like to watch wrestling too, huh," Christian assumes, pulling out the box of cereal and gallon of milk, as she's witnessing Lil' Devin using the kitchen's table as the wrestling ring for his action figures, "Believe it or not, I'm actually a huge wrestling fan myself. John Cena is my favorite wrestler and, I used to like Shawn Michaels as well, when he used to wrestle. How about you, Lil' Devin, do you have a favorite wrestler?"

"Yes, Triple-H is my favorite," Lil' Devin gleefully replies with a sparkle in his eyes, overly excited that someone else in this house is as big of a wrestling fan as he is.

"Cool, I like Triple-H as well, Lil' Devin," says Christian, carefully placing the bowl of Fruity Pebbles in front of Lil' Devin on the dining room's table, "Maybe after you're doing eating your breakfast, we can watch one of the wrestling DVD's your mom has out there in the living room."

"Yeah, I'd like that," Lil' Devin responds, after swallowing a spoonful of his favorite cereal.

As promised, right after Lil' Devin has used his spoon to scrape out the remaining pieces of Fruity Pebbles in his bowl, him and Christian are heading toward the living room area to watch Wrestlemania-25 on DVD.

All throughout the day today, Monica has called several times to check up on Lil' Devin and Christian, to make sure everything is ok. Each time she's called, Christian appears to have had everything under control, which eases Monica's stress level tremendously.

"Well, I should be home shortly, Christian," Monica explains during her last phone call for today, before leaving her job at St. Ambrose Medical Center, "I'm stopping at the Chinese joint on my way home, would you like for me to bring you anything to eat?"

"Yes indeed, girl," Christian replies, "A box of shrimp fried rice will work for me!"

"Sure thing," Monica concludes, "Tell my baby I'll see him when I get home this evening.

For the past few weeks, things seem to be working out find when it comes to Monica, Devin and Christian's living arrangements. By Christian living at Devin and Monica's house, she's been saving them some money of not having to send Lil' Devin to Daycare anymore. Surprisingly enough, a friendly bond has also surfaced between Christian and Devin. Instead of just speaking as they past one another in the house, they've actually been discussing some interesting political topics recently. Every once in awhile, Monica will throw her little two cents in on these highly debated topics, although it's perfectly clear that she has no clue what she's talking about.

"Babe, how about we play a few hands of cards," Devin suggests, wiping off the dining room's table in case Monica accepts his offer.

"Where did you put the deck of cards at, Devin?" Monica replies, momentarily walking away from the stove fast enough to find the cards then, returning to her crisp fried chicken that's cooking.

"Tell me where they are, Devin," says Christian, walking over to offer her assistance, so Monica won't burn up the chicken that she's preparing for dinner, "I got it, Monica, you can just focus on our food, honey."

"Why thank you," Monica laughs, "You two can play a few hands without me, I'll be over there to join you when I'm finished in the kitchen."

Last year sometime, when Monica first became employed as a Nurse's assistant at the Medical Center she works at now, she opted in to be an on-call type of employee, because her and Devin desperately needed the money to pay off their mortgage. Fast forward to this year, the present, Monica's on the verge of opting out of this agreement because, every time she's comfortable at home, spending time with her family and/or, just relaxing in bed, the phone rings, with someone from her job calling on the other end.

"Shit, this happens every time," Monica raves, angrily slamming the hand of cards she's been dealt down on the table, "I shouldn't even answer it because, I'm honestly not even in the mood to go to work tonight."

"I told you several times already, Monica," Devin replies, thoroughly examining the cards in his hand before making his next move, "You've been working there long enough now to be able to just work a regular 9-5 shift in the morning time. Mention it to your boss the next time you're at work."

Looking over at the Caller-ID, as the house phone begins to ring again, Monica depressingly shakes her head as she replies,

"It looks like I'll get my opportunity to do so tonight, at work."

"Damn babe, this makes 3 nights straight this week that you've been called in to work during a random time in the evening," Rodney disappointingly replies, neatly gathering the deck of cards together to place them back in the box, "You definitely need to have your schedule adjusted as soon as possible."

"Aw, does my baby miss me at night when I'm not beside him in bed?" Monica hugs Devin from behind while he's still seated at the dining room's table, passionately kissing him on his neck.

"It's not just about me, Monica," Devin claims, too embarrassed to express how he really feels, "Your son needs to have you home at night as well."

"Babe, Lil' Devin is usually asleep at night when I leave out for work," says Monica, pulling her purple-colored scrubs out of the closet to iron out before heading into the bathroom to take a shower, "But, I will mention it to my boss tonight that I need to change my schedule."

"Yeah, ok," Devin briefly responds, pushing his chair underneath the table, as he's heading toward the bedroom, "I'll catch you in the morning, Christian."

"All right, Devin, goodnight," says Christian, deciding to head to bed herself.

After taking a brief shower and getting dressed for work, Monica's glancing at herself in the bathroom's mirror, cautiously snapping her ear-rings in both ears, before heading into Lil' Devin's room to give him a kiss.

"Mommy will see you in the morning, baby," Monica softly whispers, gently kissing Lil' Devin on his forehead, as she turns to exit his bedroom.

Having already made Devin aware a few minutes ago that she's leaving out, Monica's exiting the comfort of her darkened house, trading this atmosphere in for the stressful graveyard shift that St. Ambrose Medical Center is waiting to present her with.

Its 2:00 a.m. now and, Devin is making his way into the kitchen to get something to drink to quench his late night thirst. Any other time, Devin would already have his tall pitcher of water or juice on the nightstand in the bedroom, right next to the bed. However, by Devin being so frustrated last night over Monica's constant overnight shifts that she's been assigned to work, Devin headed into the bedroom last night without his afterhours refreshing drink by his side.

"Damn, all of the Mountain Dew soda is gone already," Devin utters, thoroughly searching through the cold refrigerator for the next best thing to drink, "Hell, I guess I'll have to settle for this pineapple soda since it seems to be the only thing we have left in here to drink."

Titling the 2-Liter bottle of soda over his empty pitcher, until every drop has been released, Devin's discreetly fondling his sac, as if he has to use the bathroom now.

"You don't have to do that, Devin," Christian softly replies, standing in the corner of the hallway, observing Devin from a room's distance, "I'll handle that for you."

"Oh, shit, you scared the hell out of me, Christian," Devin flinches, almost dropping his pitcher of soda to the floor when Christian made her presence known, "What will you handle for me though?"

"Your dick, Devin," Christian boldly replies, as she's walking closer toward Devin, "I saw you fondling it a minute ago; you shouldn't have to do that yourself, let me do it for you."

"You're out of your damn mind, Christian," Devin urgently responds, walking toward a different area from where he was previously standing in the kitchen, "Monica will kill my ass and yours too, if she found out that something was going on between us."

"Ah, I guess you're not the tough man I thought you were after all," Christian provokes, persistently following Devin with each step he's making, "You're afraid of what your little wife might do to you."

"I'm not afraid of shit," Devin claims, poking his chest out with pride, attempting to defend his dignity as a man, "I'm just not fucking around on my wife."

Not taking no for an answer, Christian has gravitated within arm's reach of Devin, forcefully stunning him with a kiss on the lips, defiantly testing his loyalty to Monica.

"Come on now, Christian," Devin attempts to resist, "Why are you trying to get some shit started in here?"

"I'm just attracted to you, boo," Christian seductively purrs, holding Devin's face between her hands, "I've been having these feelings for you ever since we locked eyes a few years ago at that cookout my family had."

"I stand too much to lose though, crossing the boundary lines with you."

"You'll only lose something if Monica finds out about us," Christian persuasively mutters, sliding down on her knees, releasing Devin's stiffening penis from the slit of his football imprinted boxers, "I don't plan on mentioning anything to her, do you?"

Too weak to put up a fight any longer, Devin's using his left hand to place his cold pitcher of soda on the counter, while his other hand freely dictates the gravitating motion of Christian's bobbing head. Peeping around the wall that separates the kitchen from the hallway, Devin's paying close attention, making sure Lil' Devin doesn't wake up and races out into the kitchen area to catch them in the act.

"Fuck yeah, just like that," Devin moans, allowing his boxers to slide down even further, enabling his entire sac to slam aggressively against Christian's mouth and chin.

"Scoot back a bit, babe," Christian dictates, using Devin's strong arms to rise up in a standing position, "I want to feel this big dick deeply inside of me before I carry my ass back to bed."

Doing as Christian says, Devin's bare naked ass is flush against the kitchen's counter, as he's anxiously waiting to see the position that Christian wants to be annulated in.

"No, come over this way, boo," Christian passively pulls Devin by the arm, "When I bend over in the sink, I want you to slide your huge penis deeply inside of my wet pussy."

On this particular night, this ground breaking turn of events that occurred between Devin and Christian, lasted way longer than expected. On several occasions, Devin had Christian in multiple compromising positions on the sink and counter area, when he ravishingly pounded his large member piercingly into her anatomy.

However, by the expressionless demeanor written on both of their faces this morning, while they're sitting at the dining room's table having a cup of freshly brewed coffee with Monica, you'd think that nothing took place between these two last night.

"So, did you speak to your boss about adjusting your schedule, honey?" Devin replies, not giving Monica eye-to-eye contact as he speaks.

"Yeah, my new schedule will be in effect starting this Friday, sweetie," says Monica, gently massaging her throbbing temples, "No more of this overnight shit for me."

"I know that's right, girl," Christian mutters, as she's carrying the coffee mugs over to the sink to wash them out, "That graveyard shift would wear my ass out too."

"Where's my baby, Devin," says Monica, "He must be really tired if he's still asleep this late in the morning."

"No, he's in his room playing the video game, babe."

"Cool, let me go in here to speak to my baby before I lay down to get at least a few hours of sleep."

"I'm right behind you, love," Devin replies, sticking closely to Monica so she really won't pick up on the slightest hint of what occurred last night.

Ever since that unpredictable occurrence in the kitchen last night between Devin and Christian, things appear to have transformed itself back to how it was before between these two, in the beginning. Not much is being said as far as an on-going conversation.

At the most, a simple, hello, is as far as their dialogue goes.

Nevertheless, life has a tricky way of presenting repeated situations to us, sometimes in the same atmosphere, same predicament, testing our human will against untimely temptations. It's Thursday night and as usually, Monica's being randomly called in by her job to work the overnight shift for the last time before her new 9-5 schedule goes into effect tomorrow.

"I'll see you guys in the morning," Monica replies, her weary eyes giving off an appearance like she hasn't had a decent amount of sleep in days.

Monica's off to work now, Lil' Devin is over his grandma's house, so, this leaves Devin and Christian in another uncompromising situation all over again. Any other time, whenever Monica's home, Christian respectfully wears the type of clothing that covers her body parts up completely. However, by Monica not being home again tonight, Christian's letting it all hang out, literally. Devin's in the living room at the moment, watching the basketball game, not focusing on anything else other than that. Quite naturally, this lack of attention isn't sitting well with Christian, so, as a result, she's entering the living room area as well, wearing some silk black-colored boy shorts and a matching tank-top, allowing her huge breasts to spill out from the sides.

"Damn, babe," Devin immediately responds, a tad bit slower than his awakening penis does, "You look sexy as fuck with that shit on!"

"So, you like, huh?" Christian playfully shakes her huge wiggling ass from side to side, causing Devin to lustfully reach out for it.

Meanwhile, as Devin and Christian are apparently about to get into another steamy-hot, unforgiving night of sex; Monica is surprisingly being released from her job way earlier than planned. Her boss hired a few more people this week, enabling Monica to go back home and climb into her warm, cozy bed until she has to report back to work tomorrow morning.

"I wish someone would've at least called me at home to tell me I didn't have to come in tonight," Monica complains, throwing her pocketbook over her shoulder, as she's heading out of the Medical Center.

The drive home this time of the night is a clear shot for Monica. Half of New Jersey is fast asleep, causing the streets to be almost empty tonight, with fewer drivers on the roadway than normal.

"I can't wait to get in my bed," Monica yawns, mashing down on the eject button of her CD Player in her car, waiting for the CD to slide out so she can put another one in.

Pulling up in the empty parking spot across the street from her house, Monica's carefully parallel parking, making sure she doesn't accidentally bump into the car that's in front of her the slightest bit, or the one behind her either. Gradually opening the driver's side door after successfully parking, Monica notices a car she hasn't seen in this neighborhood before, parked directly in front of her house, the very spot where she usually parks her car.

"I wonder who that car belongs to," Monica mumbles within, aiming the keyless remote at her car to lock the doors, as she's proceeding toward her steps.

Turning to take one last glance at her car, making sure the front lights are lighting up at the same time the horn blows, symbolizing that the car doors are safely secure, Monica is seemingly about to be ambushed by the guy exiting the mysterious car that's parked in front of her house.

"Oh my goodness, Mike, what are you doing around here!" Monica immediately panics, racing up the steps of her house, anxiously fidgeting with her keys.

"You know exactly why I'm here, bitch," Mike angrily replies, urgently racing up the steps behind Monica, "Where's that scandalous ass cousin of yours?"

Opening the front door of her house just in the nick of time, Monica stumbles in the hallway, quickly turning around to slam the door before Mike enters the house behind her.

"Christian, hurry up and come out here," Monica nervously yells, crawling on the floor, as she's rushing toward the bedroom, "Your husband, Mike, has found out where you are and he's at my front door threatening to harm me!"

Clumsily opening the door of her bedroom in search of Devin, or anyone else who can possibly help her at this point, Monica is devastatingly shocked, as she opens the bedroom's door completely, only to find Christian mounted on top of Devin in her bed, giving him the ride of his life.

"What the fuck!" Monica yells at the top of her lungs, pouncing on top of Devin and Christian on the bed, as she's wildly swinging with detrimental intentions.

"I'm out here busting my ass at work at night, trying to make a living so we can afford this fucking house, Devin, and this is what you two have been doing behind my back!"

"Babe, I'm sorry, just calm down for a minute so I can explain things," Devin fearfully replies, grabbing Monica from behind, as he's attempting to pin her down to the bed.

"I can't believe your ass, Christian," Monica loudly cries out, trying to escape Devin's firm grip, "I'm your fucking blood, your cousin, the one who gave you a place to stay when your husband was beating your ass! How could you do this shit to me, me of all people?"

"I'm so sorry, Monica, I swear I am," Christian progressively tries to plead her case, as she's backing up toward the front door of the house, extending her hand out to Monica, "Please find it in your heart to forgive me for what I have done to you."

Forgetting all about Mike being on the opposite side of the front door, anxiously anticipating his opportunity of getting his hands on his wife, Christian, again, Christian is immediately reminded of Mike being on the porch, when a piercing bullet burns through the door, entering the back of Christian's skull, exiting the front of it with the same amount of force.

In a matter of minutes, Christian's lifeless body drops to the floor, almost as fast as Mike's escape from the scene was.

"Oh my goodness, he fucking killed her!" Monica painfully yells, finally escaping Devin's grip, as she's lingering over her deceased cousin in the hallway.

After these horrific incidents occurred that night, Monica hasn't spoken a word to Devin ever since.

A Legal Joint Custody agreement was established by these two, giving both parents an equal amount of time that's to be spent with Lil' Devin, but, that's it; no other type of communication outside of this whatsoever. Mike, was eventually arrested this summer after being caught by the local police department, during a bank robbery that took place at the Bank of New Jersey, about a month ago. From my understanding, Mike was sentenced to the maximum of 30 years to life, with no parole. By Christian not having any close relatives outside of Monica, a funeral never took place for her. Her body was eventually cremated not too long after her death.

Often times in life, we ignore the important fact that, our actions and decisions we choose to make in life, ultimately not only affects us, but, the affect extends even further to those whom we may be close to and/or involved with relationship wise. In Tammy's case, she witnessed multiple uncalled for ordeals occurring within her mom, (Sharon's) house as a kid growing up, resulting in Tammy mimicking a few of these treacherous traits herself. Like most kids these days, Tammy's dad was elusive in her life as well, causing her to grow up into her adulthood, craving for this unfulfilled void that she's carrying around with her, to be fulfilled by someone who's showing the least bit of interest in her. However, if and when Tammy finds this man of her dreams, will it honestly be a dream come true or, a nightmare that will change her life completely?

Sitting at the kitchen's table, inhaling her 6th Newport cigarette from the pack, Sharon's scattering through a table full of bills that she has no clue of how she's going to pay off. Her new boyfriend, Roger, is unemployed at the moment, but, has a strong lead on filling a possible position that's available at Mills Lumber Company, if he's hired for employment.

"Baby, I'll be right back," Sharon anxiously replies, quickly fastening the zipper of Tammy's jacket, guiding her 6-year-old daughter toward the front door, "I'm almost out of cigarettes so, I'm going to the corner store real quick to get another pack."

"If you have enough money on you," Roger utters, pouring the last remaining drops of lemonade that's left in bottle, into his tall glass, "Can you bring me a beer back as well."

Totally disgusted that she had to sit at the table a minute ago, scrapping up enough money for cigarettes and now, she's being asked by a sorry excuse for a man if she can bring him a beer back from the store, Sharon's exiting the house without even responding to Roger's request.

"Come on, Tammy," says Sharon, rushing up the street to the local convenient store, battling with the strong gusty winds in her effort to make it to her destination, "Walk a little faster before this heavy snow and strong winds blow us away from here, sweetie."

"Ok, mommy, I'm walking as fast as I can," Tammy replies, briefly turning her head away from the forceful winds that's showing no mercy to anyone this cold winter's evening.

"All right, sweetheart, stand right here for a moment," Sharon instructs, pointing to the exact spot that her daughter is supposed to stand, "Mommy's going to buy her cigarettes and use the pay phone, then we'll be heading right back to the house."

Although Tammy's only 6-years-old at the current moment, she's still having inquisitive thoughts of who her mom can be calling on the pay phone right now. Whoever it is, her mom, Sharon, appears to be extremely happy to hear from them, by the huge smile on her face.

"Mom, was that my dad on the phone?" Tammy softly replies, looking up at her mom, hoping she'll give her the answer she's been waiting on.

"Girl, hush up and come on here," says Sharon, blatantly ignoring Tammy's question, as she's guiding her by the arm, rushing her out of the convenient store.

Since Tammy's question wasn't directly answered right away, she wondered all the way home if that was her dad on the other end of her mom's conversation and if not, why hasn't he been around to see her lately. Tammy never did receive the answer to her question verbally, however, her question was answered indirectly on several occasions, by the different amount of men she's witnessing her mom allowing into their home whenever Roger isn't around. Ironically enough, Sharon claims that each and every one of these new faces is one of Tammy's uncles whenever she introduces them to Tammy. Tammy isn't aware of how big her family really is but, she honestly doesn't feel as though these different guys are legitimate members of it.

This routine continued on and on over the years within Sharon's house, way into Tammy's teenage years. Tammy never got the chance to see her dad show her mom tons of love and affection like she hoped she would someday, but, almost every other night, Tammy had no other choice other than to witness a different man show his lustful affection for her mom. The nights when Tammy didn't see it, she'd hear it loud and clear, by how loudly her mom screamed and moaned in the room right next to hers, during her sexual encounters with these random guys. Roger was history years ago as far as his relationship with Sharon. Roger wasn't generating any type of income which meant his time living here was limited to begin with.

"Baby girl, I want you to always remember one thing," Sharon explains to Tammy, combing her hair one night while they're sitting in the dining room alone, "As you continue to grow up into your adulthood as a full grown woman, always be extremely careful with the selection of guys you choose to align yourself with. Except nothing less than respect from them at all times and never deal with anyone whom you can't prosper with on most levels, if not all. Don't follow in my footsteps, Tammy, by doing the things you might see me doing; don't follow in my footsteps at all, sweetie."

This conversation between Tammy and her mom, Sharon, took place right here in this living room where I stand, about 9 or 10 years ago. Ever since that eerie evening of Tammy coming home from school to find her mom slumped over in the living room's chair dead, with a needle still stuck in her arm, no other tenants has leased this apartment since. Too many dreadful memories still lingers around in this place preventing Tammy from renting it herself but, she does live a few blocks up the street now, with her boyfriend, Lamar, whom she's been with for the past five years. Lamar recently completed his sophomore year in Georgetown University and plans to return next semester to finish up on obtaining his degree in Social Studies.

Tammy, on the other hand, has her very own hair salon that's located about twenty minutes from here, on the corner of Milton Ave and Barkley St. Starting her own business wasn't an easy task at all and, if it wasn't for Tammy's hustling mentality combined with the street pharmacists she's dealt with before her and Lamar became an item, it's no telling where Tammy would be at this stage of her life.

Waiting impatiently at Penn Optical this morning, for his prescription glasses to be ready for pick-up, Lamar's restlessly flipping through the pages of a couple of magazines that are scattered on the table in front of him. It's a fairly brisk day outside today weather wise so, Lamar's dress attire on this particular day consist of denim colored jeans, a yellow polo shirt, butter timbs and his sky-blue framed colored glasses that are about to be replaced by the medicated glasses he's here for.

"Sir, you can step right over here," one of the employees explains, as she's waiting for the payment of Lamar's glasses. "How will you be paying today, Sir, cash or credit card?"

"Oh, my insurance will cover the bill," says Lamar, politely handing his insurance card over, as he's adjusting his glasses on his eyes, "While you're at it, when you hand my receipt over to me, make sure your phone number is being passed over as well."

"My phone number," the young lady quietly replies, "Why would I pass my phone number over to you?"

"It's the only way I'd be able to call and find out what time I should pick you up for dinner this weekend," says Lamar, in a cool confident tone.

Meanwhile, at Tammy's Hair Salon, Tammy's going on and on about the loving man in her life, Lamar.

"Girl, don't you know when I got home from work night before last, my man had dinner prepared and my bath water ran for me already," Tammy brags, stepping back a few steps to admire the beautiful hair style she's just blessed one of her clients with.

"Damn, are you serious, girl?" Tammy's top employee, Leila replies, as she's escorting her client over to her booth. "I'd give just about anything to find me a man that does those type of things and who is all about me!"

"Trust me when I tell you," Tammy continues, "My boo is one of a kind."

Not buying a minute of it, Tammy's other employee, Renee, is assertively putting her two cents in on this conversation.

"Boss lady, I respect you and all," Renee begins, comfortably taking a seat, as she's waiting for her next client to come in, "But, I honestly don't think your man is any different from the rest that's out here. I mean don't get me wrong, Lamar might spoil you from time to time by doing nice things for you and all, but, deep down inside, that brother has a bit of deceit in him just like everyone else."

"You see," Tammy defensively replies, washing her hands thoroughly, as she's glancing in the mirror to respond, "The negative energy that you're presenting to me, Renee, is something that I can't get with."

"Oh, I'm not being negative at all, Tammy; I'm just keeping it real."

"Oh, really now," Tammy embarrassingly mutters, "Tell me again how long have you been in your relationship, Renee."

"You know I'm not in one, Tammy, and it's perfectly cool with me. I choose to remain single so I won't have to deal with the bullshit I've dealt with in past relationships. However, since you've lucked up and found Mr. Right, you go right ahead and enjoy every minute of it. I honestly do hope that things work out for the best; you deserve it."

"You're damn right I do," Tammy boastfully responds, as if she's putting the final imprints on this conversation, "That's exactly why I've been blessed enough to find a man who'll never turn his back on me; I deserve it. Lamar loves me, I love him and nothing will ever tear us apart; nothing or no one."

"Amen my sister," Renee sarcastically claps, pissing Tammy off even more in the process, "You tell it like it is!"

Even though Renee's words actually did get under Tammy's skin quite a bit, Tammy refuses to let it show. Instead, her embedded game face is still intact, not showing any signs of her being the least bit worried about Renee's assumptions. To put this all behind her, Tammy just made her way into the break room area a minute ago, apparently pulling out her cell phone to give her man a call.

"Hey, honey, how's your day going so far?" Tammy replies, holding the phone closely to her ear, peeping around toward the door at times to make sure no one's coming.

"My day is going pretty good," Lamar replies, "I just left Penn Optical, now I'm on my way downstairs in the mall to pick up a few more things, babe."

"Make sure you pick up something for me," Tammy smiles, rising up out of the chair as if she's heading back to work now.

"Oh, for sure, baby," Lamar utters, "You know your man is going to look out for his sweetheart."

"I love you baby," Tammy seductively replies, "I'm going back to work now, I only have another hour left and I'll be off but, I wanted to hear your voice for awhile."

"You'll hear it even more when I get your ass in bed tonight," says Lamar, instantly wetting Tammy's panties with the slightest words that come out of his mouth.

Smiling from ear to ear, Tammy's heading back out amongst her employees and clients, to proceed with her daily working tasks.

"Aw, she's glowing," Leila smirks, as Tammy's entering the work area, "She must have been back there on the phone talking to Lamar."

"Girl, whatever," Tammy blushes, signaling with her hand for her next client to come over to her booth, "Rosaline, I'm ready to start on your hair now."

Later that evening at home, things in the bedroom are transpiring exactly how Tammy anticipated them to. Lamar's deep penetration in bed is knocking every ounce of stress out of Tammy's body that accumulated during the course of her long work day earlier today.

"Baby, you take such good care of me," Tammy moans, firmly cinching her nails into Lamar's hairy chest, as her wide hips slowly begins to grind while she's on top of him, "No other man has ever made me feel the way you make me feel."

"That's because I take pleasure in pleasing your ass," Lamar progressively roars, sliding his manly hands up Tammy's medium sized frame, beginning with her flat, ring pierced stomach, ending up with a delicate stroke of both of her swollen protruding nipples.

Intensified love making between these two continued on throughout the night. Whenever Tammy dosed off and, Lamar felt his penis becoming erect again, he'd slide it right back in her, a few times while they were both lying on their sides. Any position is fine with Tammy though. As long as she's enjoying the sensation of having her man's prime Grade-A Beef stuffed deeply in her anatomy, no complaints were coming out of Tammy's mouth.

"What a wonderful night we had last night, babe," Tammy rolls over to kiss Lamar, as the radiant sunlight beaming through the curtains of their bedroom, defiantly makes its presence known.

"Yeah, it was so good I don't even feel like going to work today," Lamar replies, wishing he had another free day under his belt so he could miss a day's work at Sean's Clothing Store.

"Aw, I didn't mean to put it on you that good, boo," Tammy laughs, forcing herself up out of bed to take a shower.

Groggily turning over to see the time on the digital clock that's on the dresser, Lamar notices Tammy's cell phone vibrating on the floor, next to the bed. At the moment, Lamar's laying motionlessly, debating on if he should invade Tammy's privacy by roaming through her cell phone to see who just called her this early in the morning. When these two first met, Tammy had a gang of dudes on her heels daily trying to get with her. She made Lamar aware of this from the start and has claimed that she has no involvements with any other guy outside of Lamar. In the back of his mind, Lamar knows that he runs this same type of game on women, making them feel like they're the only woman when in reality, they're not. It just has him contemplating at this point, wondering if Tammy's running the same game on him now.

Nevertheless, instead of nosily roaming through Tammy's unguarded cell phone, Lamar's crawling over to his own phone to check the missed calls that he couldn't answer last night. While doing so, Tammy just turned the water off in the bathroom, meaning she'll be returning to the bedroom at any moment now, so, Lamar's fingers are moving extremely fast at the moment, checking his missed calls before Tammy walks into the room.

"Say, honey," Tammy utters from the bathroom area, gradually drying off, as she's walking into the quiet bedroom to finish, "I have a clinic appointment this morning and, two clients that wants their hair done today as well. What do you say to a movie tonight?"

"Hold on, one thing at a time, babe," Lamar replies, as he's sitting on the edge of the bed, "What's the clinic appointment about?"

"It's nothing major, silly," Tammy chuckles, "Just the normal girlie check-up."

"Cool, you had me puzzled there for a minute," Lamar sighs, sliding his bedroom slippers on, as he's heading toward the bathroom, "If not tonight, I'll definitely take you up on that movie offer tomorrow night, babe."

"Do you already have plans for tonight, Lamar?"

"If so, it'll just be with the guys, babe, shooting some pool like we normally do on Friday nights," says Lamar.

"Don't get fucked up in here, Lamar," Tammy rolls her eyes, reiterating the thoughts that Renee planted in her mind yesterday about how most guys are unfaithful, "You're not lying to me, are you?"

"Now who's being silly now?" Lamar laughs.

Recalling a few chapters she read in Steve Harvey's book, "Act Like A Lady, Think Like A Man," Tammy's quietly beginning to compare it to Lamar's actions, curious to see if she can catch him in a bald face lie.

Tammy executed this strategy all the way up until it was time for her to leave out for today, but to no avail. Everything she asked, Lamar followed right up with a prompt answer. By Tammy witnessing so much as a young kid growing up, most things right under her mom's roof, other random but important things on her own, enables her to be very street smart within her own rights. The only problem with that is, she's dealing with a man in Lamar, who can also claim his fair share of street savvy because, he grew up in a rough and rugged neighborhood just like Tammy has. Being slick with his words, especially when it comes to women, is the reason why Lamar's out on his first date with the young lady he met at Penn Optical yesterday, Regina, while Tammy's under the impression that he's out shooting pool with his buddies, Marvin and Steve.

"Let's take the seats over there in the corner," Lamar suggests, taking Regina by the hand, as he's leading her toward a dark secluded section of the restaurant.

"Look at you, acting like you're hiding from someone," Regina shakes her head, glancing over her shoulder, following the motion of Lamar's roaming eyes, "Are you involved with someone, Lamar, if so, we can leave now?"

"Baby, I've already explained that I just got out of my relationship last month sometime," Lamar exclaims, "It's no one else besides you."

"We'll, you need to start acting like it," Regina rolls her eyes.

"All right, baby, I will, starting now," Lamar playfully smirks.

Using the same methodical method he uses on Tammy and any other woman he's designated as his prey for the evening, Lamar's pulling out all of the moves it takes to get Regina back to her place tonight. At first, Regina declined the offer, claiming that it's too early for anything other than something as innocent as dinner and a movie. Due to Lamar's exhausting persistence though, she's shockingly submitting to the idea of spending some time at her apartment this evening.

"Now, I hope you're not involved and some dude randomly shows up while I'm in here with you," says Lamar, using the reverse psychology method to throw Regina off track.

"Psstt, I told you I'm single, Mr. Playboy," Regina smiles, turning the key to her front door with Lamar a few steps behind her.

"Damn, baby, this is a nice place you have here," Lamar quietly compliments, surveying the entire apartment with his eyes, in search of any signs of a man's clothing, "How long have you been living here?"

"Not long, roughly five or six months."

"Ok, you have a beautiful home, babe," says Lamar, as he's walking closer toward Regina, "But, you know for a fact that it's nowhere as beautiful as you are."

"You're such a charmer," Regina mutters, bashfully battering her eyes, "Are you this way with all the girls?"

Immediately interfering with the numerous amounts of questions that Regina would like to ask, Lamar has bee-lined straight toward her neck, kissing it in an aggressive manner that has Regina melting in the palms of his hands.

"I'm going to do things to you that no man has ever done before," Lamar predicts, ravishingly ripping Regina's clothes away from her succulent skin.

Tenderly positioning Regina across her queen-sized bed, face first down in her fluffy pillows, Lamar's slowly pulling his long penis out of the confines of his brief bikinis, blocking Regina's extending hand that's reaching for the condom that's lying on the bed next to them.

"We don't need this, baby, you're safe with me," Lamar utters, tossing the condom to the floor, far away from Regina's sight, "I want you to feel me tantalizing your G-Spot while I'm completely raw."

"I don't want to get pregnant though," Regina initially bridges up to stop Lamar in his tracks.

"You won't get pregnant, baby," Lamar softly nibbles on Regina's ear, causing her to lifelessly flop down on her satin sheets when his large penis inserts her secretion, "Daddy wants to take real good care of you tonight, that's all."

Just as he'd planned, that one lustful night with Regina, in her bed, on the living room's floor, even out on the patio of her apartment, has Regina blowing his phone off the hook. By Lamar showing both women, Tammy and Regina, the same amount of love and affection that both of them obviously lacked from their fathers in their lives, it's extremely hard at this point for either woman to catch on to the fact that Lamar's playing them both.

For Lamar, at this stage in his life, things couldn't be going any better. He's on the verge of obtaining a lucrative career after he graduates from college this year, he has a beautiful home, two beautiful women and things couldn't be better. This all remained true until today at 12:47 p.m., when Lamar received an irate phone call from Regina, claiming that she went to the clinic last week for her annual check-up and it turns out that she's HIV Positive.

"Get the fuck out of here, Regina," Lamar panics, unable to finish washing his car after being hit with this bombshell, "Who did you get it from because I sure as hell don't have anything?"

"Lamar, you're the only fucking guy I've been with since my last annual check-up," Regina cries, completely devastated of the fact that, one night of unprotected sex with Lamar has changed her life completely.

"I don't fucking believe this shit," Lamar angrily flings his cell phone toward the trashcan that's on the corner, "Now I have to get tested myself and on top of all of that, I have to explain this shit to Tammy. Man, my life is fucking over!"

A couple days later, after building up enough courage to get tested as well, Lamar's results turned out in the same heartbreaking fashion that Regina's did.

"Sir, I'm sorry to be the one to break this news to you today," Nurse Samson replies, as she attempts to comfort Lamar a bit, "However, we do have advanced treatments for this condition these days and, I'd be more than happy to talk with you about the options we can make available to you."

"Ma'am, it's no way that test can be accurate," Lamar continues to rave, pacing back and forth in the hallway of the clinic, "It's just no way that this can be happening to me."

"Again, Sir, I'm sorry."

Storming out of the hospital, not wanting to accept the dreadful fact that's been brought to his attention today, Lamar decides to head home and isolate himself away from the world, at least until he gets his head clear.

"I just can't believe this shit," Lamar loudly cries out, firmly clenching locks of his hair, as he's down on his knees in his bedroom, "It's like a fucking nightmare that I just can't wake up from."

While being in the midst of his heartache and pain, Lamar's startled a bit when he hears a soft knock on his front door. Lamar has every intentions of ignoring it, whoever it is couldn't possible bring him any good news to erase this life changing ordeal he's faced with. The only thing that's causing him to wipe the tears from his eyes and head downstairs to answer his door is, Tammy's voice, repeatedly asking Lamar to let her in.

"It's opened, Tammy," Lamar softly replies, unlocking the door but, quickly walking away from it, "Turn the knob and let yourself in."

"I've been ringing your phone off the hook all morning, Lamar, why didn't you pick up and answer me?" Tammy replies, as she's entering Lamar's house.

"I just didn't feel like being bothered, Tammy, that should've been obvious to you by now."

"Listen, Lamar," Tammy begins to explain, remaining close to the front door with a look of guilt taking control of her face, "I already know what you're going through, your friend, Marvin told me about it a few minutes ago. I know it's nothing I can say that'll change things or, that'll make you feel any better at all. I also know how you're feeling right now and I totally understand if you can't find it in your heart to forgive me."

"Forgive you," Lamar intervenes, attentively posturing himself to get a clearer understanding of what Tammy's trying to explain, "How could you possibly know how I'm feeling right now, Tammy?"

"Lamar, like I was trying to say," Tammy continues, slowly cracking the front door opened, while she's talking to Lamar, "A few years ago, I was told that I'm HIV Positive as well, but, I . . ."

Without getting a chance to finish her sentence off, Tammy urgently takes off running toward her car, with Lamar in hot pursuit of her.

"Bitch, you mean to tell me that I'm going through this shit because of you and you weren't even woman enough to tell me!" Lamar furiously yells, continuously kicking the side of Tammy's car door, until she zooms off down the street.

Lamar never saw Tammy again after that day. She obviously knew that her life was in even more danger now, so, she decided to relocate elsewhere. However, both Lamar and Regina have been receiving treatment regularly and have been coping with this illness very well. Lamar has also become a spokesman for other people worldwide that are experiencing this same type of illness. His messages strictly exemplify the importance of abstinence or, using protection during sexual intercourse, each and every time.

Regina has been silent on her behalf and chose not to speak openly about this subject matter.

Interlude
~ For Every Action, They'll Always Be A Reaction ~

Very seldom in relationships/marriages, when the love for one another has finally ran its course, instead of some couples throwing in the towel, mutually agreeing to go their separate ways, they'll remain in the marriage/relationship, just to continue to play the 'see-saw game' with their partner. To further explain what I'm referring to when I say, 'see-saw game', this term simply means that, when one person does something out of line to violate, frustrate or piss off their partner, their partner will keep this cycle going by retaliating, doing the same in return or, maybe even something worse. As a result, things we keep going back and forth, up and down, as both members of the relationship/marriage jockey's for better leverage over their partner. Some might refer to this trend as 'tic-for-tack,' while others categorize it as simply getting even. Whatever the case may be, who does it really benefit in the end?

Anyway, now that I've briefly touched up on that topic a bit, let's continue to move right along to the next topic. For me, growing up from my adolescence straight into manhood, I've always been the type of person who's been fully aware of the value that lies within family. This cruel world that we live in is hard enough on its own, trying to manage and survive the best way that we can. During these times is when we're supposed to be able to look toward our family for love, understanding and support. Unfortunately, while this might work out perfectly for some, others find themselves confining in a complete stranger during rough times, more than they can with their own family members.

The term I'd often hear, 'blood is thicker than water,' has subsequently become a trampled over cliché, time and time again, as family members continues to betray and/or turn their backs on each other. Take a good look at story number three; highlighting what took place inside of Monica and Devin's home. Monica demonstrated her loyalty toward her family in the beginning, when Christian was being abused by her husband and had no one else to turn to other than Monica. As a reward for showing her hospitality and genuine concern for a family member that's going through rough times, Christian ultimately stabs Monica in the back by sleeping with Monica's boyfriend, Devin.

Now, this situation was the ultimate sign of disrespect and a lack of remorse. Christian was actually bold enough to fuck her cousin's man, right inside of her cousin's house, in her cousin's bed, after her cousin was the one who provided a place for her to stay to keep her safe. This is a prime example of what it means to not be able to trust anyone, if your own blood/family would do you this way. The only good part about this terrible dilemma is; Monica and Devin's son, Lil Devin, wasn't around when things really unfolded that night. Witnessing the horrific scenes that occurred within his mom and dad's house that evening would've definitely scarred Lil Devin for the rest of his life. Lives were literally destroyed that night with one ending in an unexpected fatality. Even though Monica and Devin will probably never see eye-to-eye again on anything, at least Lil Devin hasn't been deprived of not being able to spend an equal amount of time with both of his parents, although I'm sure he'd prefer to do it as a united family once again. It seriously has a deep affect on a child whenever he/she is used to see their parents together then, all of a sudden, for whatever reasons, a separation between the two takes place.

When this occurs, the child involved will somehow find a way to vent, letting out his/her frustrations of not seeing their parents together anymore. Their mood and behavior will often times drastically change, in school, at home or anywhere else the child isn't usually disruptive at. That's why it's extremely important that time is mutually spent with both parents and, whenever the parents are together in the presence of the child, they are to put their differences aside for the moment and present a mature, moderate toned atmosphere, even if they can't stand each other deep inside. The child is always the most important factor in this equation and they don't deserve to have to go through or, witness the drama themselves.

The last story I shared with you all, depicting the relationship between Lamar and Tammy, is hands down one of the most serious stories from the four that I've shared within this book. These days in time, for whatever reasons, some of us are still blinded to the fact that our partners, being a relationship, marriage or, just friends with benefits, sometimes has other sexual partners that they're dealing with as well. Never, under any circumstances, allow yourself to just let down your guards, walking around in life being naïve, assuming that your partner isn't being sexually involved with anyone else outside of you. On very rare occasions, this assumption is true. I'm not saying that everyone cheats because; it might be a few out here in the world today that doesn't cheat. What I am saying is, always expect the unexpected. We're all human and from time to time, some of us might fall victim to temptations. Trust me, I've been there and done that throughout my life. What we are to do though is learn from our mistakes so we won't keep repeating them over and over again. You might be a person that's the bill of health so, why risk that for someone who has the potential of putting your life in danger by not using protection; especially when you know you're being cheated on?

Nevertheless, in Lamar and Tammy's case, Tammy grew up witnessing her mom live her life in a trifling manner to begin with. Tammy's father was never around and, in his place, a different man would appear just about every other night in her mom's bedroom. This is another example of how our ways and actions can leave a lasting impression on our kids, good and bad, depending on what we're exposing them to. Tammy saw it all living under her mom's roof and, unfortunately, some of those bad habits rubbed off on Tammy and remained with her all the way into her adult life. Tammy knew all along that she was HIV positive but, never parted her lips once to make her boyfriend at that time, Lamar, aware of it. Not to say that Lamar was innocent in this relationship either, because he wasn't. He was probably affected years ago, by having unprotected sex with Tammy on several occasions, but, he just wasn't aware of it.

As a result, Regina and anyone else for that matter that Lamar was cheating with outside of his relationship, was exposed to the same illness that Lamar was exposed to by Tammy. That's how this detrimental trend continues to affects us daily. The slogan, 'If it affects one of us, it affects us all," is the absolute truth. In a few minutes, I'll elaborate further on the different types of STD's that are being transmitted, the risk factor of each, as well as the current statistics that goes along with them. Like I stated at the beginning of this book, in no way, shape or form am I trying to offend anyone with these facts that I'm providing. I'm just putting out an effort to make readers more aware of these serious situations and illnesses, to deeply educate the mind. Before I elaborate on that topic, let's look into the steps most people go through after the relationship/marriage has ended and, while everyone recovers from a breakup differently, I'll also give my input and suggestions on a few key steps that can be taken that seemed to help me move on from my past relationships.

Five Grieving Stages After the Relationship Ends

When experiencing a painful blow to our emotions and hearts, due to a relationship/marriage coming to a definite end, we quite naturally feel an immediate void and a sense of loss of someone or something we grew accustomed to having. To help assist you with the understanding of the 5 main stages of grief you'll most likely feel when you and your former partner decides to go your separate ways, I've summarized them below for you to study and compare them with the actions that occur in your lives after the relationship/marriage has ended. Note, not everyone will experience these stages in the exact chronological order I've listed them in. However, after reading each stage in depth, compare it to a past relationship of yours and see if you remember encountering these feelings within. Afterwards, I'll also explain a few key steps I've taken myself in the past to help me move on with my life after the relationship has ended.

1. Living In Denial

Anytime we're presented with something as heart-wrenching as a relationship/marriage abruptly ending, we often times have an immediate numb reaction to the situation. We hear the person we're involved with, breaking things off in the selective manner that they choose, but, at the same time, our minds doesn't always fully accept the fact that it's really over. In these cases, you might find yourself saying that, you feel like you're having a nightmare that you can't wake up from.

2. The Bargaining Routine

In the midst of attempting to shake off the numb feeling we're experiencing after hearing the person we're involved with, breaking things off, most of us rush right into the next stage, which is the bargaining method, in an attempt to get the relationship back on track once again. Some will agree to eliminate certain friendships they may have had during the course of their relationships that their partner didn't necessarily get along with. Others will promise to do better individually, making any needed changes within that will accommodate their partner much better. Sometimes, by the time this level is reached, your partner most likely will already have in their minds that it's nothing you can say that'll make them stay in the relationship/marriage any longer. If they do decide to do so, the end result can very well still turn out to be heartbreaking for you because, this was basically a forced situation.

3. Anger Takes Control

No one enjoys the feeling of being rejected. You'd be surprised at the alarming amount of people in this world today that are doing things that's way outside of their comfort zones, just so they can be accepted by society, peers and the person they're intimately involved with. However, when all of these things are executed and the results are still leading to rejection, anger takes full control over some people, causing them to vengefully lash out in retaliation. The blame game comes into play and, the partner/person that's rejecting you, will be called every derogatory name in the book. The personal secrets they've revealed to you during the course of the relationship will be exposed at this point. You're fighting dirty now and won't feel any better until they're hurting as well.

4. Depression Soon Follows Up

An emotion we feel inside as humans that can very well go hand-and-hand with anger is, being depressed. During this stage, you'll find yourself being isolated from things you'd normally do. For some, an immediate appetite change will come into affect where as though, you'll find yourself either eating too often or, not really eating anything at all. It has finally began to sink in that, the relationship/marriage is really over and, it's nothing you can do in your power to change that. It's somewhat of a hopeless feeling inside, blatantly robbing you of any control you may have had over things before in your life. Recognizing this depression stage in your life after the marriage/relationship has ended is extremely important. I say this because it enables you to begin to take tiny steps on your pathway of recovering emotionally and moving on with your life. But, if this deep depression feeling lingers on too long and you began having thoughts about doing some harm to yourself or, someone else, this is the wise time to seek help, to assist you on getting back on the right track. Don't allow yourself to do anything that'll lead to you harming yourself or others and end up being in trouble or, resulting in a fatality. Its life after the relationship/marriage has ended and, you deserve to experience every bit of it.

5. Finally Accepting Things For What They Are

After you've experienced the previous four stages when the relationship/marriage has ended, you'll eventually reach the level where you'll find yourself accepting things for what they truly are. Your rational ability of thinking will become clearer and, you'll be back on track of moving forward with your life.

Healing and Moving On With Your Life

Thoroughly enduring the Top 5 Stages I've just provided about the feelings you'll experience after the breakup first occurs, will undoubtedly lead you right into the next set of stages, 'Healing and Moving on With Your Lives.' It wasn't easy for me to follow up on these things myself at first but, after precisely executing each step in my own pattern and in my own time, I found myself pleased with the end results.

1. Getting The Grieving Emotions Out

In life, we'll always be faced with some type of circumstances that'll cause us to grieve (Being the death of a loved one, relationship/marriage ending, etc.) Keeping these feelings confined within us is not healthy at all. My advice is to let it out, even if you have to do so privately. Those whom suppress their feelings about a breakup, never allowing themselves to grieve, are the ones who'll most times never fully learn the lessons that are to be learned from this circumstance.

2. Never Fall Victim To The Self Pity Syndrome

All right, the relationship/marriage has ended and quite naturally, you're feeling the painful affects of it in the beginning. However, never allow yourself to beat yourself up about what could've/should've been done differently to extend the relationship.

The changes that you may see at this point that could have been adjusted were to be done during the course of the relationship still existing. Once it has ended, accept that and move forward at your own pace. Embrace the lessons learned from the former relationship/marriage and revise the personal issues you see within yourself that needs to be adjusted before entering another relationship.

3. Don't Turn To Alcohol To Ease The Pain

Sometimes, we can be presented with so much stress, agony and frustrations in life that, it causes some of us to turn to alcohol to ease away the pain. Unfortunately, using alcohol to drain away the pain we're feeling inside can actually make things worse. The next morning, after you've sobered up, your problems still exist and quite naturally, the pain hasn't subsided completely either. On top of the problems you're already faced with, now you've added another issue onto your list by potentially becoming an alcoholic, if your newly found drinking habits continues.

4. Journalize Your Feelings

While this method might not be appeasing to most, some will find it beneficial to jot down your feelings about the relationship/marriage ending, on a piece of paper or in your note pad. You'd be surprised at the numerous amounts of discoveries you'll unfold by trying this method.

5. The Replacement Theory

After the relationship/marriage has ended, some will immediately rush right into another one with someone else. I can honestly admit that I've done this before myself. Dealing with other people does assist in removing your ex from the brain, but, you have to also analyze the fact that you're dealing with someone new now, possessing new issues for you with the new problems of their own you'd have to adapt to. Saying this, it's probably a wise decision to not rush right into another relationship as your avenue of getting over the one that just ended. You need more than enough time to learn the new person's ways so you won't end up making things worse for yourself than they already are.

6. Love Yourself

After the breakup occurs, now is the time to do the things that you love to do in life. Try to at least give yourself a month or so to do the things you enjoying doing (spending time with friends, shopping, taking long walks, working out, etc.). This is the perfect time to build a stronger, wiser, healthier you before attempting to step back into the equation of potentially entering another relationship.

As I stated before, these steps that I've provided doesn't necessarily have to be done in the exact order I've listed them in. We're all different and have different methods and time frames of moving on with our lives after a relationship/marriage concludes.

Now that we've covered the basis on those important factors, let's move on by taking a deep look into the different types of sexual transmitted diseases that we put ourselves in risk of contracting by not using protection with our partners. I'll also provide the symptoms and statistic rate for each STD I talk about.

Sexually Transmitted Diseases

Sexually Transmitted Diseases are, illnesses that has a significant probability of transmission between humans by means of human sexual behavior, including vaginal intercourse, oral sex, and anal sex. In the past, these illnesses were mostly referred to as STDs or VD. However, in recent years, the term sexually transmitted infections has been preferred, as it has a broader range of meaning. A person may be infected, and potentially infect others, without showing any signs of a disease. Now having explained this, we should get a clearer understanding of the risks we're taking each time we have unprotected sex with our partners. Don't think by a long shot either that, all because a person looks good as far as their physical appearance that they're completely clean health wise either because, that's far from the truth. Accept it or not, even our very own partners, the ones we sleep with on a regular basis in our relationships/marriages, are risks factors as well.

Even if you're being 100% faithful yourself, doesn't necessarily mean that your partner is practicing the same thing (man or woman). One of the main problems with some people today is their lack of accepting things for what they really are. I've run across several young ladies within my lifetime who are claiming that their men will never cheat on them. They've subsequently forced themselves into believing that their relationships are exclusive, their men wouldn't dare cheat on them with anyone else so, there's no point in using protection. Sadly enough, this is one of the main reasons why our country ranks at the top of the list statistic wise, when it comes to new cases of STDs/STIs being transmitted. Both genders, men and women, are cheating.

There's a diverse amount of different STDs/STIs I can highlight within this book, but, this time I'm only going to focus on a couple of them. As you're attentively reading through each one, consider taking higher measures of protecting yourselves during sexual intercourse if you're not doing so already.

1. Syphilis

Syphilis is a highly contagious disease spread primarily by sexual activity, including oral and anal sex. Occasionally, the disease can be passed to another person through prolonged kissing or close bodily contact. Although this disease is spread through sores, the vast majority of these sores go unrecognized. The infected person is often unaware of the disease and unknowingly passes it on to their sexual partner.

Pregnant women with this disease can also spread it to their baby. This disease, called congenital syphilis, can cause abnormalities or even death to the child.

Syphilis was once a major public health threat, commonly causing serious long-term health problems such as arthritis, brain damage, and blindness. Signs and symptoms of syphilis include a firm, round, small and painless sore on the genitals, anus, or mouth, or a rash on the body, especially on the palms of the hands or the soles of the feet.

If diagnosed in its early stages, syphilis can very well be treated. If it's not treated, it may then progress to a stage characterized by severe problems with the heart, brain and nerves. This year alone, 2011, Syphilis cases hit a 30-year high of 347,000, a 62 percent spike over 2009.

2. Chlamydia

Chlamydia is a bacterial infection disease transmitted when people have sexual intercourse. It is the most common sexually transmitted disease in the United States, with over 2.8 million affected individuals each year. Among adults, about 5% of the population is estimated to be infected. Among sexually active adolescent females, about 10% are infected. Chlamydia is transmitted in 2 different ways:

A. From one person to another through sexual contact (oral, anal, or vaginal).
B. From mother to child with passage of the child through the birth canal.

Chlamydia is also known as a "silent" disease because the majority of infected people have no symptoms. In women, bacteria initially infect the cervix and urethra (urine canal). Women who have symptoms might have an abnormal vaginal discharge or a burning sensation when urinating. If the infection spreads from the cervix to the fallopian tubes, some women still have no signs or symptoms; while others have lower abdominal pain, low back pain, nausea, fever, pain during intercourse, or bleeding between menstrual periods.

Men with signs and symptoms might have a discharge from their penis or a burning sensation when urinating. Some men might also have burning and itching around the opening of the penis. Pain and swelling in the testicles are uncommon.

3. Gonorrhea

Gonorrhea is a sexually transmitted disease caused by Neisseria gonorrhoeae (a bacterium that can grow and multiply easily in the warm, moist areas of the reproductive tract, including the cervix, uterus and fallopian tubes in women and, in the urethra in women and men. The bacterium can also grow in the mouth, throat, eyes and anus. Gonorrhea is another common infectious disease and it's estimated that more than 700,000 people living in the United States get new infections each year. Gonorrhea is spread through contact with the penis, vagina, mouth, or anus. Ejaculation does not have to occur for gonorrhea to be transmitted or acquired.

People who have had gonorrhea and received treatment may get infected again if they have sexual contact with a person who's infected. Symptoms and signs include burning sensation when urinating, or a white, yellow, or green discharge from the penis. Some men with gonorrhea get painful or swollen testicles.

In women, the symptoms of gonorrhea are often mild, but most that are infected have no symptoms at all. The initial signs and symptoms that does occur include a painful or burning sensation when urinating, increased vaginal discharge, or vaginal bleeding between periods.

Symptoms of rectal infection in both men and women may include discharge, anal itching, soreness, bleeding, or painful bowel movements.

4. HIV

Human Immunodeficiency Virus (HIV) is a lentivirus that causes
(AIDS) Aquired Immunodeficiency Syndrome, a condition in humans
in which progressive failure of the immune system allows life-
threatening opportunistic infections and cancers to thrive. Infection
with HIV occurs by the transfer of blood, semen, vaginal fluid, pre-
ejaculate, or breast milk. The four major routes of transmission are
unsafe sex, contaminated needles, breast milk and transmission from
an infected mother to her baby at birth.

Most untreated people infected with HIV-1 eventually develop AIDS.
These individuals mostly die from opportunistic infections or
malignancies associated with the progressive failure of the immune
system. HIV progresses to AIDS at a variable rate affected by viral,
host and environmental factors. Most will progress to AIDS within 10
years of HIV infection; some will have progressed much sooner and,
some will take much longer. Without antiretroviral therapy, someone
who has AIDS typically dies within a year.

The most common symptoms include fever, lymphadenopathy,
pharyngitis, rash, myalgia, malaise, mouth and essphageal sores and
may also include, but less commonly, headache, nausea, vomiting,
enlarged liver/spleen, weight loss, thrush and neurological symptoms.

In 2009, it was estimated that there are 33.3 million people worldwide
infected with HIV and this staggering number has grown even more
since then.

Quite naturally, the list can continue on of different STDs/STIs that are infecting most people in the world today. For now, I only wanted to briefly touch up on the four that I've named and, save the others for another title I plan to share with you all in the near future. Within this book, I'm hoping that you'll walk away with some very informative knowledge after reading through the pages. You might even be able to openly discuss some of the topics this title provides, with a relative and/or close friend of yours. Before I let you go, allow me to summarize things up from what we've learned from this book when it comes to detecting your spouse deceitful, unfaithful behavior, cracking the cheater's code once and for all.

Cracking the Cheater's Code

If there ever comes a time that you have a gut feeling that your partner is cheating on you, don't ignore that feeling. Ignoring our instincts and second guessing ourselves and thoughts, often times come back to haunt us. Your partner has shown you something within their character, mood swings, or change of personality that's causing you to feel as though their cheating. Something is definitely different about them and maybe you can't pinpoint what it can be right away. Well, from my past experiences and I'm sure I'll learn even more as my life continues, I'll share with both genders (male and female) what signs to pay close attention to, that'll lead you to cracking the code of a cheating spouse.

Guys:

If in the beginning, your woman may have become easily irritated and/or angry because of certain things you may have done or didn't do, but now, all of a sudden, she's happy go lucky about everything (including the bad things), this is a huge sign to pay close attention to. Unless she's going through a serious transition in her life that's causing her to not really give a damn about what you do, good or bad, it's another underlining reason behind this. A change in a person's behavior is one of the top things to always pay attention to. If you're not making them be this happy then, someone else must be doing so.

Next, if the two of you used to have the type of relationship/marriage where as though you could talk openly about anything, but, she's become more secretive lately, this is another sign to pay attention to. It's important to find out and to understand the reasoning behind her deceitful, sneaky/secretive demeanor that's causing you to have to ask about certain things now when at first; it was voluntarily shared with you by her.

Now, with the cell phone situation, this can work for either gender. If phone calls aren't answered around you or, you notice that the ringer is never on while you're in his/her presence, a sign of guilt is right underneath your noses with this one. If there's nothing to hide when it comes to either party in the relationship/marriage, why do private calls have to always be taken? Even if nothing is being done by your partner to violate your relationship, you'd sure feel that way by how sneaky they're acting when it comes to phone calls being made or continued in your presence. For a person that's cheating, text messaging is a vital instrument to use. You can always keep track of the person/people you're being unfaithful with, without even picking up the phone to carry on with an extended conversation. Again, keep in mind that, not everyone who texts regularly is a cheating person. They could very well have a legitimate reason for having to do so. It's up to you to pay attention to your partner though, especially if you feel as though you're being cheated on.

Guys, this is the last one for us then I'll educate the ladies a bit further as well. Dress appearance is crucial in many ways. If you have the provocative dressing type of woman who loves to flaunt what she has by wearing see through clothing, low cut blouses and short mini-skirts, keep in mind that, the same thing you see when she walks out of the house like that, is what other guys see as well.

If you're the type of guy that trust your woman 100% and you see nothing wrong with her wearing these things, so be it, more power to you. For me, a respectful boundary line has to be drawn from the start, making her aware, if she doesn't already know, of what's appropriate to wear out into the public and what's not. Otherwise, I'd always have the notion that this is blatantly being done to attract attention from others outside of the relationship/marriage, for whatever reasons.

Ladies:

Always keep in mind that, the eyes never lies. If your man is the type that has roaming eyes, showing you no respect whatsoever by looking at other women, even while being in your presence, you can imagine what's being done when you're not around. This goes for women too though. Females have a slick way of checking out other guys, but, will make it appear as if they aren't. Like I say, the eyes never lies so, pay close attention to them.

Next, if you're interested in a guy and you'd love to have as much of his time and attention that you can possibly get, but, his time is extremely limited when it comes to you, chances are, he's already involved. For both male and female, the ones who are involved, but still date other people outside of the relationship as well, they'll always give the majority of their time to the main person they're involved with. You'll get to see them and spend time with them when it's convenient for them but, that's usually as far as it'll go. Another thing that'll make you aware of this is, never being allowed to spend time with them at their house.

They'll often request to spend time with you at your house but, you're never allowed to come to theirs. That's because they're already involved and wouldn't dare take the risk of bringing you to their place of residence where the main chic or main man resides as well. I'm sure anyone who reads this book will be able to identify with something I've said as far as cracking the cheating person's code. If not, now you have some valuable information under your belt to use to your advantage now.

In closing, although none of us wants to be hurt by revealing the fact that we're being played for the fool by the person we love, it happens all of the time and will unfortunately continue on as long as this world exist. I'd be lying to you if I claimed that things will change for the better when it comes to infidelities because, in actuality, they'll probably get worse. If you do choose to get involved in a serious relationship, always have the mindset that you'll be wise enough to always expect the unexpected. Never put anything past anyone; we're all human and most of us fall quickly under temptation faster than others do. Don't be naïve saying what can't/won't happen to you because, it will, in the blink of an eye. If you're not emotionally built for the heartache and pain that comes from the games people play these days when it comes to relationships/marriages, I advise you to just stay single and have friends. Whatever you do, single or in a relationship and even marriages, make sure you're always using protection.

God Bless You All and Until the Next Time, Be Safe . . .

Signed,

Jerome Staten

Acknowledgements

As always, it's extremely important to me that I thank our Heavenly Father first and foremost, for blessing me with the gift of writing and for allowing me to learn so many different things on my journey. This is (Novel/E-Book) number four that I've released so far and, I plan to continue to release even more in the near future. To everyone who has spent their hard earned money to support me by purchasing this title, I'm very appreciative of you and I hope you've enjoyed this book from the beginning to the end. Also, I have to dedicate this book as usual to those who are near and dear to me, my family and my companion. Jerome Jr., Ja'ron and Jasmine, I love you all from the bottom of my heart. To my mother and aunt, I'm extremely appreciative of you beyond measures. Also, to my grandmother (who's deceased now), may you Rest In Peace and, I hope I'm continuing to make you proud even in spirit. To my readers and supporters, that would like to contact me personally, come to my Facebook Page and select the "Send E-mails Directly To Jerome Option." I'll be waiting to hear from you.

~ God Bless ~

Jerome Staten

www.facebook.com/jeromestaten

Are you interested in purchasing other merchandise provided by Jerome Staten? If so, all of the info is provided below!!!

(Other Books by Jerome Staten Available on Amazon Kindle)

Daddy's Sex Chronicles- Volume One

Daddy's Sex Chronicles- Volume II "Special Edition"

Burning Bridges- The Sandra Davis Story

We're Living in the Last Days

(Audio-Book and CD Available on iTunes & Amazon MP3)

Daddy's Sex Chronicles (The Audio-Book) Saga 1-6

Getting Dirty After Dark (The CD) 8 Tracks

Join Jerome Staten On Facebook Today!!!

(www.facebook.com/jeromestaten)

Shop for Women's Clothing & Adult Items

(www.flawlessbyjay.com)

www.ingramcontent.com/pod-product-compliance
Lightning Source LLC
Chambersburg PA
CBHW051837040426
42447CB00006B/579